铜仁学院 2022 年度博士科研启动基金项目（trxyDH2209）研究成果

A Study of Teacher Support on Students' Learning Effects in a Blended Learning Environment

混合学习环境下教师支持对学生学习效果的影响研究

杨 婷 著

湘潭大学出版社
XIANGTAN UNIVERSITY PRESS

图书在版编目（CIP）数据

混合学习环境下教师支持对学生学习效果的影响研究 = A Study of Teacher Support on Students' Learning Effects in a Blended Learning Environment : 英文 / 杨婷著. -- 湘潭 : 湘潭大学出版社, 2024.3
ISBN 978-7-5687-1301-6

Ⅰ. ①混… Ⅱ. ①杨… Ⅲ. ①高等教育—教学研究—中国—英文 Ⅳ. ① G649.21

中国国家版本馆 CIP 数据核字 (2023) 第 233154 号

混合学习环境下教师支持对学生学习效果的影响研究

A Study of Teacher Support on Students' Learning Effects in a Blended Learning Environment

杨婷 著

责任编辑：倪慧燕
封面设计：李　平
出版发行：湘潭大学出版社
社　　址：湖南省湘潭大学工程训练大楼
电　　话：0731-58298960 0731-58298966（传真）
邮　　编：411105
网　　址：http://press.xtu.edu.cn/
印　　刷：长沙创峰印务有限公司
经　　销：湖南省新华书店
开　　本：880 mm×1230 mm 1/32
印　　张：7.25
字　　数：274 千字
版　　次：2024 年 3 月第 1 版
印　　次：2024 年 3 月第 1 次印刷
书　　号：ISBN 978-7-5687-1301-6
定　　价：49.00 元

序

考虑到英语水平对个人发展和国家发展的重要性，以及中国英语学习者的整体英语水平，教师支持对学生的学习投入和学习成果的影响变得日益显著。此外，混合式学习已成为高等教育中一种较为盛行的教学方法。因此，本研究旨在探讨在混合学习的环境下，教师的情感支持、认知支持和自主支持这三种不同类型的教师支持对中国英语学习者在学习投入、语言学习态度和听力水平方面的影响。

国内的66名大学生参与了该个案研究。参与者为大学三年级学生，均参与了为期17周的混合式课程学习。本研究采用了“前测－课程实施－后测”的准实验研究设计。为了比较不同类型教师支持对学习者的影响程度，我们将参与学生随机分为三组，分别为情感支持组（ES，22人）、认知支持组（CS，22人）和自主支持组（AS，22人）。在课程实施期间，教师对各组学生进行相同的混合式英语课程教学，分别给不同小组施以不同类型的教师支持行为。

在前测之前和后测之后，分别对学生进行了结构化问卷调查，旨在检验不同学生的学习投入和学习态度在不同类型的教师支持行为的影响下是否产生了改变。同时，为了检验学生的英语听力水平是否会因为教师支持行为的类型不同而产生变化，所有的学生在课程实施前和课程实施后需要分别参加大学英语四级的听力前测和后测。

本研究主要有以下发现：第一，关于教师支持对英语学习者学习投入的影响，研究发现教师的情感支持对提高英语学习者的行为投入、认知投入和情感投入均有显著效果；教师的认知支持和自主支持对提高英语学习者的行为投入和认知投入都有显著效果。此外，通过比较不同小组间的影响效果发现，教师的自主支持比教师的认知支持在提高英语学习者的行为投入上有更显著的效果；教师的认知支持比教师的情感支持和自主支持更有利于提高外语学习者的认知投入。此外，三种类型的教师支持在提高学生的情感投入上具有相似的效果。

第二，关于教师支持对英语学习者学习态度的影响，研究发现三种类型的教师支持均能显著提高学习者的自信心，而三种类型的教师支持在缓解学生的语言焦虑上都有显著的正向影响。此外，在提升学生的自信心方面，教师的自主性支持比教师的情感支持和认知支持更为有效；而在缓解学生语言焦虑方面，教师的情感支持比教师的自主支持和认知支持更为有效。

第三，关于教师支持对英语学习者听力水平的影响，本研究发现教师的情感支持、认知支持和自主性支持对学习者的英语听力水平均有显著的促进作用。此外，教师的自主性支持和认知支持比教师的情感支持更能有效地提高学生的英语听力水平。

基于上述发现，本研究为英语教师在混合式学习环境中实施教师支持提供了新的教学启示，即有必要将教师支持这一概念视为一个多维结构。同时，最好将三种类型的教师支持（自主支持、认知支持、情感支持)结合起来,进而满足学生在自主性、关联性和能力方面的基本需求,从而激发学生的学习动机,获得更好的语言学习成果。

最后,衷心感谢韩国世翰大学的金锣英教授和李池莲教授在本研究中给予的帮助和支持。没有她们的建议和指导,我不可能完成这项具有挑战性的研究工作。她们对研究和工作的奉献精神和态度也为我成为一名合格的教师和研究者树立了榜样。

Preface

Considering the importance of English proficiency in personal and national development and the overall English proficiency level of Chinese EFL learners, teacher support becomes more obviously and positively influencing students' learning engagement and improving their learning achievement. In addition, blended learning has become a prevalent instructional method in higher education. Therefore, the current study aimed to examine the effects of three different types of teacher support, teacher's emotional support, cognitive support and autonomy support, on Chinese EFL (English as Foreign Language) students' learning engagement, language learning attitude, and listening proficiency in a blended learning environment.

66 university students in China participated in the current study. The participants were all junior students enrolled in a 17-week blended course. The study used a quasi-experimental research design with a pretest-treatment-posttest structure. To compare the extent to which participants were randomly influenced by different types of teacher support, they were divided into three groups, which were assigned as the emotional support group (ES, n = 22), the cognitive support group

(CS, n = 22), and the autonomy support group (AS, n = 22). Each group took the same blended English course and was given different types of teacher support during the experimental period.

Structured questionnaire-based surveys were conducted before the pre-test and after the post-test to examine whether there are any changes in students' learning engagement and learning attitude as a result of different types of teacher support. Similarly, to investigate whether there are any changes in students' listening proficiency as a result of different teacher support types, all participants were required to take the CET listening tests as the pre-test and post-test before and after the experiment.

The major findings of the current study are as follows.

Firstly, regarding the effects of teacher support on Chinese EFL students' learning engagement, it was found that teacher's emotional support is significantly effective in improving EFL students' behavioral engagement, cognitive engagement, and emotional engagement; teacher's cognitive support and teacher's autonomy support are both significantly effective in promoting EFL students' behavioral engagement and cognitive engagement. In addition, in comparing the effects between different groups, it was found that teacher's autonomy support performs more significant in enhancing EFL students' behavioral engagement than teacher's cognitive support; teacher's cognitive support is more beneficial for EFL students to improve their cognitive engagement when compared with teacher's emotional support and autonomy support in respective. Moreover, three types of teacher support have a similar effect in enhancing students' emotional engagement.

Secondly, as for the effect of teacher support on Chinese EFL students' learning attitude. It was found that all types of teacher support can significantly improve students' self-confidence while all types of teacher support have a significant positive effect on reducing students' language anxiety. In addition, in terms of self-confidence improvement, teacher's autonomy support is more effective than teacher's emotional support and cognitive support. While in terms of reducing students' language anxiety, teacher's emotional support is more effective than teacher's autonomy support and cognitive support.

Thirdly, regarding the effect of teacher support on Chinese EFL students' listening proficiency, it was found that teacher's emotional support, cognitive support, and autonomy support can all be significantly effective in promoting students' listening proficiency. Moreover, compared to teacher's emotional support, teacher's autonomy support and cognitive support are both more effective in improving students' listening proficiency.

There are several pedagogical implications grounded on the above findings. The current study provided new insights on the implementation of teacher support in an EFL blended learning setting, suggesting that it is necessary to view teacher support as a multidimensional construct. In addition, it might be better to combine the three types of teacher support, which could satisfy students' basic needs for autonomy, relatedness, and competence to stimulate students' motivation and gain better language achievement.

Finally, I would like to express my sincere thanks to Professor Kim Na-young and Lee Jiyon of Sehan University for their help and support during this study. Without their advice and guidance, I think I could not accomplish this challenging work. Their dedication and attitude to research and work tell me what a qualified teacher should be like.

CONTENT

第一章　导论

本章主要提出了在现行的混合式教学模式逐渐兴起的背景下,研究教师支持对学生学习成果,尤其是英语学习成果的影响的必要性;同时提出了本书研究的主要问题,即在混合学习环境下,教师支持对英语学习者在其学习投入、语言学习态度、听力水平方面是否存在影响。本书将围绕上述三方面对作者实施的教学过程及研究结果进行分别阐述。

Chapter 1 Introduction

1. Background

As the most important lingua franca, English, crossing national and cultural boundaries, has been spoken by people with different native languages (Yu, 2016). In addition, as a key component of one's own human capital, English proficiency also plays a vital role in international communicative activities and international trade (Firdmuc, 2016). Regarding the importance of English in personal and national development, English has long been part of the curriculum for most students in non-English-spoken countries. English as a Foreign Language (EFL) refers to the study of English by non-native speakers in countries where English is not the dominant language (Nordquist, 2020). Different from learners of English as a Second Language (ESL), EFL learners do not have enough chances to practice and improve their language proficiency in their daily lives as ESL learners do (Longcope, 2009). Thus, classroom has become an important place for EFL learners to learn and practice their language proficiency (Khajavy et al., 2018).

Foreign language proficiency refers to the knowledge and abilities to use another language to listen, speak, read and write in a situation

(Yamashita, 2002). When learning a language, "proficiency is the ultimate goal of all language learning" (Nisbet et al., 2005, p. 101). In China, English is one of the compulsory curriculum for students to learn from their elementary school (Zhuang & Chen, 2017). In order to examine Chinese university EFL students' language proficiency, Yan and Gu (2020) investigated Chinese EFL students' language proficiency based on the Common European Framework of Reference for Language (CEFR), learning, teaching, assessment, which stated that Chinese university EFL students' listening proficiency level is lower than their other language proficiency level when they are freshmen and sophomores. Students majoring in English are part of Chinese EFL learners, they have more opportunities to use English in classroom and school, but it seems that their listening proficiency is still lower than their reading, writing, and even speaking proficiency (Zou et al., 2012).

In addition, language proficiency is also viewed as students' learning achievement, which can be influenced by many factors (Wang et al., 2019). For instance, student's learning anxiety, self-confidence, learning motivation, and learning engagement can influence students' academic achievement (Asakereh &Yousofi, 2018; Gan, 2020; Luan et al., 2020; Piechurska-Kuciel, 2011). Particularly, supports provided by family, peers, and teachers can also impact their language proficiency (Luan et al., 2020). Moreover, these supportive relations have direct influence on students' learning engagement and achievement (Deci et al., 1992).

For children and adolescents, family support is significant in their learning achievement (Malecki & Demary, 2002). With age progress, students leave home and go to school. They are more influenced by the school environment and are no longer greatly influenced by their family and parents. In the school environment, students are equal in their status and thus peer support becomes stronger than parent support, which showing relation with students' belongings (Kiefer et al., 2015). Furthermore, students can not be separated from the guidance of teachers. Because teachers create the basic conditions and learning environment for students by curriculum design and instructional design (Dörnyei, 2001). Therefore, teacher support becomes more obviously and positively influences students' motivation and engagement, improving their learning achievement (Kiefer et al., 2015). Regarding learning a language, teacher support has been proved to be a significant role in enhancing students' motivation and language achievement (Kazemi et al., 2016).

When viewing teacher support, some scholars regarded teacher support as a multifaceted construct. For example, it might contain emotional support, cognitive support, autonomy support, instrumental support, evaluative support etc. (Black & Deci, 2000; Chai & Gong, 2013; Klem & Connell, 2004; Melecki & Demaray, 2003). No matter how many dimensions teacher support may contain, it has been pointed out that teacher-student supportive relations can directly influence students' learning engagement and achievement (Deci et al., 1992) and students with teacher support show more impressive their academic achievement than students with teacher control (Reeve, 2009; Reeve et al., 2004).

It has been demonstrated that students' learning engagement can be positively improved by increasing teacher support (Dincer et al.,

2012; Dincer & Yesilyurt, 2017; Gagné, 2003; He, 2009; Jang et al., 2010; Lee et al., 2015; Reeve et al., 2004; Yu et al., 2016). Among the previous studies, most were conducted in a conventional face-to-face environment. Some investigated the correlation between teacher support and students' learning engagement or learning achievement by non-experimental research (Gagné, 2003; He, 2009; Jang et al., 2010), some investigated the effects of teacher support on students' learning engagement and learning achievement by conducting experiment (Dincer et al., 2012; Dincer & Yesilyurt, 2017; Lee et al., 2015; Reeve & Jang, 2004; Yu et al., 2016). But few studied on its effects under the EFL context (Dincer et al., 2012; Dincer & Yesilyurt, 2017; Oga-Baldwin, 2020; Oraif, 2018; O'Reilly, 2014).

For example, Dincer et al. (2012) found that when teacher created an autonomy supportive environment, EFL students had higher level of speaking ability. Teacher's supportive behaviors were positively correlated with students' English speaking ability and learning engagement. In addition, EFL students' writing ability was also proved to be positively improved by implementing a flipped classroom with teacher support based on Self-Determination Theory (SDT) framework in a blended learning environment (Oraif, 2018).

From the previous studies, teacher support has been verified its positive effects on EFL students' learning engagement and learning achievement. But the researcher finds that there is still limited research on the effect of teacher support on EFL students' listening proficiency. Considering Chinese EFL students are weak in their listening proficiency compared to other language proficiency (Zou et al., 2012), and listening proficiency is regarded as the foundation of effective communication (Deng, 2015), it is needed to explore whether teacher support could enhance Chinese EFL students' listening proficiency.

With the fast development of technology and the application of information and new technology, blended learning has become a prevalent instructional method in higher education (Kim & Yoon, 2021). As a combination of conventional face-to-face learning and online learning, it amends the shortcomings with only one form of instruction and affords more choices for both students and teachers (Wang et al., 2019). Therefore, there have been many studies implementing blended learning into the EFL context. When blended learning is combined with EFL learning, it can not only increase students' motivation and engagement (Banditvilai, 2016; Liu, 2013; Yoon & Lee, 2010) but also develop students' language proficiency (Ginaya et al., 2018; Grgurovic, 2011; Shih, 2010).

Among those studies, the effects of blended learning have been investigated from various aspects. For example, some studies compared the effects of blended learning with conventional face-to-face learning (Banditvilai, 2016). Some studies developed an EFL blended learning model and investigated its effects on enhancing language proficiency (Grgurovic, 2011; Liu, 2013; Yoon & Lee, 2010). In addition, the effects of computer-assisted or technology-assisted blended learning in improving EFL learning were also investigated (Ginaya et al., 2018; Shih, 2010).

When blended learning becomes ubiquitous, it may also bring new obstacles to EFL students in language self-confidence because they need to share their works more frequently both online and in-class (Bailey et al., 2017). Teachers need to rethink and provide support based on the changes in students' learning attitudes and the learning environment. In this context, the definition of teacher support has been expanded. Furthermore, the requirements for teacher support have also increased (Jiang et al., 2018b).

Previous research about teacher support has been implemented either in an online environment or in a conventional face-to-face environment (Chai & Gong, 2013; Federici &Skaalvik, 2014; Klem & Connell, 2004; Liu et al., 2017). In addition, few empirical studies focused on the effects of teacher support on EFL students' learning engagement and listening proficiency together in a blended learning environment. Moreover, in the context of language learning, learners' learning attitudes, including self-confidence and language anxiety towards learning are also important in influencing language achievements (Krashen, 1982). Ghanbarpour (2016) and Tridinanti (2018) viewed self-confidence and language anxiety as a whole part to investigate language learners' learning attitudes. Since learners' self-confidence is positively direct related to their foreign language proficiency, whereas language anxiety is significantly negatively related to foreign language proficiency (Bailey et al., 2017). In addition, both self-confidence and language anxiety are important factors in the Affective Factors in Krashen's (1982) linguistic theory, which shows the importance of learning attitude in language learning. However, to date, the concurrent and systematic effects of teacher support applied in a blended learning environment on EFL students' learning attitude and learning engagement, as well as listening proficiency, have not been explored.

Therefore, to provide a more thorough analysis of the effects of teacher support in the EFL learning context, it is necessary to explore the effects of teacher support on EFL students' learning attitudes while investigating the effects of teacher support on EFL students' learning engagement and listening proficiency. The above description showed that there is a dearth of research to examine the effects of teacher support on Chinese EFL students' learning engagement, language learning attitude, as well as listening proficiency.

2. Purpose and Research Questions

The purpose of the current study is to explore whether teacher support could affect Chinese EFL students' learning engagement, language learning attitude, and listening proficiency in a blended learning environment. In particular, it focuses on exploring the effects of different types of teacher support-autonomy support, cognitive support, and emotional support-on students' learning engagement, language learning attitude, and listening proficiency.

To investigate the effects of teacher support on EFL students' learning engagement, language learning attitudes, and listening proficiency, the current study addressed the following research questions:

Q1: What are the effects of teacher support on Chinese EFL students' learning engagement in a blended learning environment?

Q1-1: Are there any changes in Chinese EFL students' learning engagement as a result of teacher's emotional support, cognitive support, and autonomy support?

Q1-2: What are the differences in Chinese EFL students' improvement on their behavioral engagement, cognitive engagement, and emotional engagement according to different types of teacher support?

Q2: What are the effects of teacher support on Chinese EFL students' language learning attitude in a blended learning environment?

Q2-1: Are there any changes on Chinese EFL students' language learning attitude in terms of self-confidence and language anxiety as a result of teacher's emotional support, cognitive support, and autonomy support?

Q2-2: What are the differences in Chinese EFL students' language learning attitude according to different types of teacher support?

Q3: What are the effects of teacher support on Chinese EFL students' listening proficiency in a blended learning environment?

Q3-1: Are there any changes in students' listening proficiency as a result of teacher's emotional support, cognitive support, and autonomy support?

Q3-2: What are the differences in Chinese EFL students' listening proficiency according to different types of teacher support?

第二章　文献综述

本章主要围绕教师支持、学习投入、语言学习态度、听力水平和混合式学习等概念进行了研究综述。尤其通过对教师支持、学习投入的定义、维度的划分,进一步明确了本书中教师支持的三种类型以及学习投入的三个维度。本章也对教师支持分别与学习者的学习投入、语言学习态度、听力水平之间的影响关系进行了分析。同时,还对在混合学习环境下语言教学已开展的相关研究进行了分析,确定了课程实施过程中的混合教学模式,进一步说明了开展本研究的必要性。

Chapter 2 Literature Review

1. Teacher Support

1) Definition of Teacher Support

Teacher support firstly appeared within the concept of social support. In Caplan's (1974) research, the concept of social support refers to the help an individual receives from the social network (family members, teachers, peers, neighbors, etc.). In the field of educational psychology, social support can alleviate the negative effects of emotions such as academic anxiety, and promote students' learning behavior and academic (Wentzel, 2017).

According to the content of support, Tardy (1985) proposed social support was a comprehensive model with emotional, informational, instrumental and appraisal support. House et al. (1988) classified social support into emotional support, informational support, evaluative support and instrumental support. According to the source of support, Ansong et al. (2017) regarded social support should contain information support, network support, emotion support, self-esteem and tangible support. While in accordance with Caplan's (1974) view, Malecki and Demaray (2002) stated that social support can be divided into parent support, peer support, and teacher support.

For children and adolescents, family support is significant in their learning (Malecki & Demaray, 2002). With age progress, students leave home and go to school where they are less influenced by their family and parents and more influenced by the school environment. In the school context, students share equal status and peer support becomes stronger, having relations with students' belongings (Kiefer et al., 2015). When comes to teacher support, it becomes obvious on students' learning achievement (Lee et al., 1999) and it affects students' motivation and learning engagement, promoting their learning and achievement (Kiefer et al, 2015).

Trickett and Moos (1973) regarded teacher support as students' perceptions of teachers' care and help. Fraser (1994) proposed teacher support meant direct structural support teachers, such as teacher-student relationship, or students' perception of teacher support. Mitchell and DellaMattera (2011) defined teacher support as providing help for learning tasks, expressing concern for students, and caring about students' interests and happiness. It is an important embodiment of teachers' active behaviors and an indispensable social-environmental variable for understanding students' academic achievement (Piechurska-Kuciel, 2011).

In Self-Determination Theory (SDT), it is believed that individuals have three basic needs, which are need for autonomy, relatedness and competence (Deci & Ryan, 2000). The need for autonomy means that people want to have their own right to do or not do something in different activities, and they want to have the right to choose and determine their behavior. The need for relatedness refers to people's desire and need to feel care and love from others so that they can see themselves as a member of a group. The need for competence refers to people having the need that they are capable to complete their tasks or work. When one's innate psychological needs in autonomy, relatedness, and competence are satisfied under the social-contextual conditions, people's intrinsic motivation will also be satisfied, which would also improve the internalization of extrinsic motivation (Ryan & Deci, 2012).

Satisfaction on the basic psychological needs can influence individuals' internalization on behaviors, which could help formulate intrinsic motivation, and consequently achieve better learning outcomes (Deci & Ryan, 2000). A study conducted by Jang et al. (2009) showed that satisfaction in students' basic needs could bring a satisfying learning experience and better academic achievement.

The school environment, as one kind of social environment, could affect individuals' satisfaction in their basic needs. Once students' basic needs are satisfied, they will perceive greater autonomy, relatedness and competence. Then they would be promoted on their intrinsic motivation, which will facilitate students more engaged in their learning tasks and gain better learning achievements (Sansone & Harackiewicz, 2000). Therefore, supporting students' basic needs are the prerequisite to improving students' intrinsic motivation and fulfilling their academic achievement. Considering this, Reeve (2009) regarded social support, especially autonomy support could significantly improve students' learning achievement.

In the school environment, teacher is the most important subject influencing students' motivation and behaviors (Stroet et al., 2013).

There have been enough studies showing that teacher autonomy support could promote students' basic needs satisfaction (Reeve, 2002), enhance intrinsic motivation (Deci et al., 1981), improve learning achievement, and maintain their learning persistence (Vallerand et al., 1997). Therefore, SDT provides a suitable theoretical framework for the present study on investigating the effects of teacher support on EFL students' learning engagement and achievement.

2) *Classification of Teacher Support*

Some studies view teacher support as a single-dimensional variable (Kazemi et al., 2016; Olani et al., 2010; Ryan & Patrick, 2001; Wentzel, 1998), while other research regards teacher support as a multi-dimensional variable (Chai & Gong, 2013; Federici &Skaalvik, 2014; Hoi & Mu, 2021; Klem & Connell, 2004; Liu et al., 2017; Tas et al., 2019). When teacher support is viewed as a single dimension, together with family support, peer support, the relations between teacher support and students' academic achievement were analyzed (Wentzl, 1998). As one kind of personal relation, teacher support had a direct influence on students' learning interests to influence students' academic achievement. Ryan and Patrick (2001) viewed teacher support as one dimension in the classroom social environment. In their study, teacher support was not uniquely associated with students' academic efficacy. Olani et al. (2010) empirically tested the effects of students' perceived teacher support and self-efficacy beliefs on their learning achievement. The result showed perceived teacher support indirectly facilitates students' statistical reasoning abilities. Kazemi et al. (2016) found a significant correlation between teacher support, students' intrinsic motivation, and English reading strategies.

Some scholars have regarded teacher support as a multi-dimensional variable that can positively influence students' learning outcomes. The content of teacher support may vary according to different contexts. For example, Klem and Connell (2004) viewed teacher support containing structure, autonomy support, and involvement and found that it could positively affect students' academic achievement. They believe that students need autonomy support from the teacher because students need to feel that they can make important decisions for themselves. If students desire the opportunity to make decisions, they also need a clear sense of structure within which to make those decisions. Federici and Skaalvik (2014) divided teacher support into emotional support and instrumental support. They studied the relationship between teacher support and students' psychological factors. Hoi and Mu (2021) divided teacher support into teacher orientation and behavior support and also suggested that students can benefit from the two types of teacher support. Tas et al. (2019) regarded teacher support as emotional, informational, appraisal and instrumental support and investigated their effects on students' learning motivation and engagement. In the study, teacher support was found to positively influence students' task-value, self-concept and engagement.

Among those different types of teacher support, teacher autonomy support is one of the most commonly researched variables. Generated from SDT (Deci & Ryan, 1987; Ryan & Deci, 2000), teacher autonomy support can help students enhance intrinsic motivation and maintain persistent interest in learning (Black & Deci, 2000). An autonomous supportive climate may positively influence students' learning engagement and achievement (Reeve & Jang, 2006).

Previous literature has proved that "the number of dimensions and the labels used for teacher support varies" (Federici & Skaalvik, 2014, p. 21). With the application of information and technology, blended learning has become a prominent method in higher education (Kim, 2021). As a combination of online and traditional face-to-face learning, it remedies the defects of a single form of instruction and provides more choices for teachers and students (Wang et al., 2019). In this context, not only has the definition of teacher support expanded, but the requirements for teacher support have also increased (Jiang et al., 2018b).

In China, considering the different social and educational backgrounds between Asian and Western countries, Chai and Gong (2013) developed a scale of perceived teacher support for Chinese middle school students and regarded teacher support as emotional support, cognitive support, and autonomy support. It was mentioned that emotional support, cognitive support, and autonomy support are the core elements of teacher support under the Chinese academic context (Chai et al., 2011). Reasons for dividing teacher support into the three dimensions had been verified by previous studies: It had been supported that teacher emotional support is important in promoting students' learning engagement, cooperation and emotional well-being (Meyer & Turner, 2007). Moreover, it had also been found that students' learning engagement, reading proficiency could also be enhanced when teachers provide cognitive support in the forms of academic challenges, feedback, stimulation on students' curiosities (Lam, 2004; Law,

2011). In addition, previous studies had found that the choice provided by teachers can be regarded as a kind of autonomy support that could positively predicate students' learning motivation, interests, and engagement in learning (Flowerday & Schraw, 2000; 2003; Flowerday et al., 2004). Liu et al. (2017) and Chi (2017) also supported Chai and Gong's (2013) view that students need teacher's emotional, cognitive, and autonomy support in the Chinese learning context. Based on the previous studies, Jiang et al. (2018b) developed the dimension of teacher support by proposing that teacher support should contain teacher's emotional support, informative support, social support and instrumental support. In Table 2-1, different dimensions of teacher support were presented.

Table 2-1 Multi-dimensions in Teacher Support

	Dimension	Researcher
Teacher Support	Emotional support Cognitive support Autonomy support	Chai and Gong (2013)
	Emotional support Informative support Social support Instrumental support	Jiang et al. (2018b)
	Emotional support Instrumental support	Federici and Skaalvik (2014)
	Teacher orientation Behavior support	Hoi and Mu (2021)
	Structure Autonomy support Involvement	Klem and Connell (2004)
	Emotional support Informational support Appraisal Instrumental support	Tas et al. (2019)

In the current study, the classification of teacher support by Chai and Gong (2013) was adopted. Considering the Chinese education context, teacher support can be divided into teacher emotional support, cognitive support, and autonomy support (Chai & Gong, 2013; Chi, 2017; Liu et al., 2017). In addition, the three dimensions of teacher support had been verified by the Perceived Teacher Support Scale developed by Chai and Gong (2013). It had also been confirmed on its feasibility and reliability in a traditional face-to-face environment (Chai & Gong, 2015) and an online learning environment (Liu et al., 2017). Moreover, students' intrinsic motivation, learning behavior, positive academic emotions and achievements will improve when their basic needs for autonomy, relatedness, and competence are satisfied (Assor et al., 2002). According to students' basic needs in psychology, it was mentioned that teachers' teaching behaviors should contain emotional support, cognitive support, and autonomy support (Chi, 2017). Therefore, it is necessary for the current study to view teacher's teacher support as emotional support, cognitive support, and autonomy support under the Chinese educational context.

(1) Teacher's Emotional Support

Under a blended learning environment, teacher's emotional support combines the features of online learning and traditional face-to-face learning, teacher's emotional support in the current study is described as the care, understanding and respect that teachers show to students through verbal and non-verbal behaviors in the process of teaching (Massey, 2010). It is a communication interaction based on interpersonal communication and technical media to enhance students' positive emotional experience to promote students' independent learning and improve students' self-regulation on their own emotions (Zhao et al. ,2018).

According to Chai and Gong (2013), teacher's emotional support refers to teachers' positive attention and care, positive encouragement, emotional understanding, confidence in believing students' competence, support on students' negative emotions when students dealing with pressure and challenges. As one of the key components of teacher support, teacher's emotional support has been regarded as teachers' dependability and showing genuine concern and respect for students, desiring to understand their opinions and feelings (Patrick et al., 2004; Pianta & Hamre, 2009). It could help students in managing their academic emotions and learning behaviors (Yeung & Leadbeater, 2010).

In Liu et al.'s (2017) study, teacher's emotional support means the teacher's positive concern for students and support in emotion when facing pressure and challenge. It pointed out that teachers should pay attention to guiding and stimulating online learners and provide positive emotional support. Specifically, teachers could provide encouragement to online learners' study, stimulate learners' motivation and learning enthusiasm, create an interactive communication climate, pay attention to learners' learning status and provide effective feedback in time. In addition, teachers need to understand the learning difficulties from learners' points of view and enlighten online learners' passive academic emotions. They could add face-to-face communication and discussion to promote learners' emotional experience.

According to Jiang et al. (2018a), teacher's emotional support refers to the emotional support that learners acquire during the course learning process, such as the teacher's sensibility to students and focus on learners' points of view. In specific, it could be performed as prompt response to learners' online message, expectation on learners' study, creating a comfortable learning climate, using humorous and emotional symbols and expressions in online communication. Jiang et al. (2018a) pointed out that teacher's active participation in students' activities could establish friendly relationships between the teacher and students. In addition, giving students prompt feedback and response could improve their feeling of belonging.

Jiang et al. (2018b) further described teacher's emotional support in the online learning environment should conclude teacher's encouragement for students to express their personal views during course learning; giving praise on students' improvement and performance; actively participating in students' after-class activities, giving suggestions on students' learning to help them build learning confidence, being able to promptly realize the difficulties that students encountered, and respecting students' response and feedback.

Based on the three dimensions of teacher support, Jia (2018) described teacher's emotional supports in a blended learning environment as participating the interaction and discussion with students and sharing teacher's point of view with students in face-to-face learning, giving comments and feedback to students' views and performance in face-to-face learning, showing interests in students' questions and points of view. According to Chai and Gong's (2013) dimension of teacher support, there have been studies listing out the operational teacher's emotional supportive behavior, which was shown in Table 2-2.

Prior studies have shown that teacher's emotional support is positively related to students' motivation and engagement (Cooper, 2013; Jin & Wang, 2019; Patrick et al., 2007; Sakiz, 2017). It could significantly improve students' self-confidence and positively predicate students' learning engagement (Jang et al., 2012; Mitchell & DellaMattera, 2011). Since the more emotional support students perceive from their teachers, the more likely they tend to show interest and persistence in learning (Yue & Lu, 2014). In addition, teacher's emotional support has been proven to reduce students' learning burnout (Zhao et al., 2018). The higher the level of teacher emotional support that students perceive, the lower their level of learning burnout.

Table 2-2 Teacher's Emotional Support Strategy and Operational Behaviors

Strategy	Operational Behaviors	Researcher
Teacher's Emotional Support	· Paying positive attention to learners' learning status · Supporting on students' negative emotions as they deal with pressure and challenges · Thinking from students' point of view · Spending time in helping students	Chai and Gong (2013)
	· Providing encouragement to online learners' study · Stimulating learners' motivation and learning enthusiasm · Creating positive learning climate · Paying positive attention to learners' learning status · Prompt response and feedback · Participating interaction and discussion with students	Liu et al. (2017)

续表

Strategy	Operational Behaviors	Researcher
Teacher's Emotional Support	· Prompt response and feedback · Expectation on learners' study · Creating positive learning climate · Using humorous and emotional symbols and expressions in online communication · Active participation into students' activities · Encouraging students to think positively, express their thought, and make autonomous exploratory	Jiang et al. (2018a)
	· Encouraging students to think positively, express their thought, and make autonomous exploratory · Giving praise on students' improvement and performance · Active participation into students' activities · Giving suggestions on students' learning · Respecting students' response and feedback	Jiang et al. (2018b)
	· Participating interaction and discussion with students · Sharing teacher's point of view with students · Giving comments and feedback to students' views and performance · Paying positive attention to learners' learning status	Jia (2018)

Ruzek et al. (2016) found that teacher's emotional support and students' behavioral engagement were significantly mediated by the effects of autonomy and students' peer relatedness experiences among middle and high school students. In specific, it proved that teacher's emotional support was significantly positively related to students' peer relatedness and autonomy, and then direct effects were found between peer relatedness and autonomy with students' behavioral engagement and motivation.

According to Jin and Wang (2019), emotional support perceived by students could be viewed as a mediator between students' gratitude and students' engagement. Together with students' basic psychological needs, teacher's emotional support was connected middle school students' gratitude with their learning engagement. Teacher's emotional support was positively correlated with students' learning engagement. Moreover, it also indicated that teacher's emotional support indirectly predicated students' engagement through the mediation of students' basic psychological needs, which indicated that when students perceived more emotional support, their needs for basic psychology could be better satisfied and then consequently enhance the degree of learning engagement.

(2) Teacher's Cognitive Support

In the study of Chai and Gong (2013), it was pointed out that teacher's cognitive support included providing academic challenges and stimulating learning curiosity (Lam & Law, 2007), providing learning strategies to improve students' academic ability and promoting students' understanding towards concepts (Richland et al.,

2007). In specific, cognitive support was contained under the five instructional components which are challenge, curiosity, real-life significance, autonomy and recognition (Lam et al., 2007). The cognitive supportive behaviors include providing students with challenging but achievable tasks, stimulating students' curiosity about the learning contents and in solving problems, giving students more autonomy in learning, linking the learning contents with students' real-life experiences, and recognizing individual efforts in learning (Law, 2011).

According to Chi (2017), it was pointed out that teachers could promote students' feeling of competence by providing positive feedback. Teacher's cognitive supportive behaviors contain providing students positive feedback and encouragement in class and after class, designing different types of learning tasks, guiding students to focus on the learning process instead of the learning results, and expressing positive academic expectations to enhance students' learning confidence.

In Liu et al.'s (2017) study, teacher's cognitive support refers to teachers providing students' academic challenges and providing relevant learning strategies or skills for students to develop their competence. In addition, teachers need to provide exercises with an appropriate level of difficulty. Under the blended learning environment, Jia (2018) mentioned that teacher's cognitive support contained discussing language learning skills with students, trying to use multimedia resources to create a language learning environment, trying to provide help when students encounter difficulties in learning.

By applying those instructional and cognitive strategies, the relationships among instructional and cognitive support, motivation, and secondary students' writing achievement were investigated (Lam &

Law, 2007). In Lam & Law's (2007) study, it was found that when students were provided with challenging tasks, autonomy, curiosity, real-life experiences, and recognition of their efforts, their learning motivation was able to be improved, then in turn, their writing achievement was improved (See Table 2-3).

Table 2-3 Teacher's Cognitive Support Strategy and Operational Behaviors

Strategy	Operational Behaviors	Researcher
Teacher's Cognitive Support	· Providing students different methods in problem solving · Providing effective feedback	Chai et al. (2011)
	· Providing academic challenges · Stimulating learners' curiosity	Lam and Law (2007)
	· Providing learning strategies to improve students' academic ability · Applying simple way to explain complex concept	Richard et al. (2007)
	· Providing students with challenging but achievable tasks · Stimulating learners' curiosity · Connecting the learning contents with learners' real-life experiences · Recognizing learners' efforts in learning	Law (2011)
	· Being good at guiding students to think instead of giving answer directly · Applying simple way to explain complex concept · Providing academic challenges · Connecting the learning contents with learners' real-life experiences	Chai and Gong (2013)

续表

Strategy	Operational Behaviors	Researcher
Teacher's Cognitive Support	· Providing academic challenges · Providing learning strategies to improve students' academic ability · Providing exercises with appropriate level of difficulties	Liu et al. (2017)
	· Providing students positive feedback and encouragement in class and after class · Designing different types of learning tasks · Guiding students to focus on the learning process instead of the learning results · Expressing positive academic expectation on students to enhance their learning confidence	Chi (2017)
	· Providing language learning skills to improve students' language aiblity · Using multimedia resources to create a language learning environment · Providing help when students encountering difficulties in learning	Jia (2018)

By students' self-reported surveys and classroom observations, it was also proved that teacher's cognitive support could significantly stimulate students' motivation to read with the result that the more cognitive support provided by the teacher, the better students tended to demonstrate in their reading ability (Law, 2011). In Xu and Carless's (2016) study, together with teacher's social-emotional support, teacher's cognitive support was viewed as cognitive scaffolding, which enabled the quality of teacher's feedback to be ensured. Teacher's cognitive support included promoting students' understanding of their learning discipline, students' self-regulated capacity, and the strategies in content learning and giving feedback. Meanwhile, it clarified the mutually dependent relationship between teacher's social-emotional support and cognitive support in the process of enabling feedback.

(3) Teacher's Autonomy Support

The concept of teacher's autonomy support was developed from the Self-Determination Theory (SDT) (Ryan & Deci, 1985). In SDT, teacher's autonomy support refers to the behaviors in which an individual in an authoritative position accepts others' opinions, identifies with others' feelings, and provides them with relevant information and choices while minimizing the use of pressure and demands (Deci & Ryan, 1985). It was defined as encouraging the process of choice and the experience of autonomy (Deci & Ryan, 1987). Ryan and Deci (2012) emphasized that individual endeavors to acquire self-determination and belongings during the process of acquiring autonomy. Once it is satisfied, one could perceive freedom as an individual. Based on the above core concepts in SDT, teacher's autonomy support was raised, in which external support was provided to create a more autonomous environment for people to fulfill one's intrinsic autonomy which could ensure the innate motivation to persist for a longer time (Chi, 2017). Under the SDT framework, teacher's autonomy support can not only have a positive relation to adjusting learners' autonomous motivation but also predicate learners' academic performance (Black & Deci, 2000).

Teacher autonomy support is a kind of interpersonal behavior that one person provides to involve and cultivate another's internal, volitional intentions to act (Reeve & Jang, 2006) and a way to nurture and support students to increase their inner recognition of their classroom activities (Reeve, 2006). It refers to teacher support which could make students feel that a) they can make important decisions for themselves, and b) the task they are assigned is relevant to their present or future lives (Klem & Connell, 2004). Teacher autonomy support is not the experience that teacher could provide directly to students. Teachers could only encourage and support students by creating classroom activities to make students perceive the support and to make students' inner motivation align with the activities (Jiang et al., 2018b).

In Chai and Gong's (2013) study, autonomy support refers to teachers give students enough freedom and support in arranging academic tasks and choosing learning content and problem-solving methods to enhance students' autonomy (Lam et al., 2009; Patall et al., 2010; Stefanou et al., 2004). It also indicates teachers' low controlling behavior, respect for students' views and feelings, and providing appropriate opportunities for students' academic activities (Skinner & Belmont, 1993).

According to Liu et al. (2017), teacher's autonomy support has the most significant influence on students' online learning engagement than the other two types of teacher support. With teachers' autonomy support, students' autonomy can be greatly promoted. It can be performed by providing students enough time to arrange learning schedules, providing diversified learning activities. In specific, providing extra educational games, practice activities to improve students' learning interests and participation, providing diversified learning resources by considering students' needs.

Table 2-4 Teacher's Autonomy Support Strategy and Operational Behavior

Strategy	Operational Behavior	Researcher
Teacher's Autonomy Support	· Accepting students' opinions · Identifying with students' feelings · Providing students with relevant information and choices	Deci and Ryan (1985)
	· Low controlling behavior · Accepting students' opinion and feelings · Providing appropriate opportunities for students' academic activities	Skinner and Belmont (1993)
	· Giving students enough freedom and support in arranging academic tasks and choosing learning content · Low controlling instructional behavior · Accepting students' opinions	Chai and Gong (2013)
	· Providing students enough time to arrange learning schedule · Providing diversified learning activities · Providing diversified learning resources	Liu et al. (2017)
	· Providing opportunities to express themselves · Low controlling instructional behavior · Providing diversified learning resources · Encouraging students to be responsible for their own learning	Chi (2017)

续表

Strategy	Operational Behavior	Researcher
Teacher's Autonomy Support	· Implementing autonomous, exploratory, and cooperative learning activities · Providing students autonomous learning resources according to teaching objectives and schedules · Adjusting teaching process according to students' autonomous learning	Jia (2018)

As for the style of teachers' autonomy support, it needs to be performed through different instructional behaviors to facilitate students' motivation. What behaviors are effective to motivate students' autonomy? According to Deci et al. (1989), autonomy-supportive teachers usually accept students' decisions instead of directing students' thinking, and also use non-controlled feedback and provide choice to students. Reeve (1999) pointed out behaviors like a) considers the students' perspectives, b) vitalizes inner motivational resources, c) provides explanatory rationales, d) uses non-pressuring, informative language, e) acknowledges and accepts negative effects, and f) displays patience as autonomy supportive behavior.

Based on this, Reeve and Jang (2006) proposed 8 types of instructional behaviors perceived as autonomy support by students: teacher's time listening to students; time giving and allowing students to work in their way; student's time talking; praise as informational feedback; encouraging students on their performance; offering hints; being responsive to student's questions; and making statements from students' perspectives. In their study, the eight instructional behaviors were positively associated with autonomy support. Likewise, there were still six instructional behaviors that were viewed negatively correlated with students' feeling of autonomy, which were regarded as the controlling instructional behaviors. It had been confirmed that the six controlling instructional behavior were the study (Reeve & Jang, 2006), it had been confirmed that students perceived the six controlling instructional behaviors as thwarting autonomy. The confirmed autonomy-supportive instructional behaviors and the autonomy-controlling instructional behaviors were shown in Table 2-5.

Table 2-5 Autonomy-Supportive and Autonomy-Controlling Instructional Behaviors (Reeve & Jang, 2006)

Autonomy Supportive Instructional Behaviors	Operational Behaviors
Time listening	· Cumulative number of seconds the teacher carefully and fully attended to the student's speech, as evidenced by verbal or non-verbal signals of active, contingent, and responsive information processing
Time allowing students to work in own way	· Cumulative number of seconds the teacher invited or allowed the student to work
Time student talking	· Cumulative number of seconds the student talked
Praise as informational feedback	· Frequency of statements to communicate positive feedback about the student's improvement or mastery, such as "Good job" and "That's great"
Offering encouragement	· Frequency of statements to boost or sustain the student's engagement, such as "Almost", "You're close" and "You can do it"

续表

Autonomy Supportive Instructional Behaviors	Operational Behaviors
Offering hints	· Frequency of suggestions about how to make progress when the student seemed to be stuck, such as "Holding the puzzle in your hands seems to work better than laying it on the table" and "It might be easier to work on the base first"
Being responsive to student-generated questions	· Frequency of contingent replies to a student-generated comment or question, such as "Yes, you have a good point" and "Yes, right, that was the second one"
Communicating perspective-taking statements	· Frequency of empathic statements to acknowledge the students' perspective or experience, such as "Yes, this is difficult" and "I know it is a sort of difficult one"
Autonomy Controlling Instructional Behaviors	Operational Behaviors
Time holding learning materials	· Cumulative number of seconds the teacher physically held or possessed the puzzle
Exhibiting solutions/answers	· The number of times the solution to a puzzle has been physically displayed or exhibited by the teacher before the student had the opportunity to discover the solution for him/herself
Uttering solutions/answerds	· Frequency of statements reveling a solution before the students had the opportunity to discover it for himself or herself
Uttering directives/commands	· Frequency of commands such as do, move, put, turn, or place, such as "Do it like this", or "Put it on its side"
Making should/ought to statements	· Frequency of statements that students should, must, have to or ought to do something
Asking controlling questions	· Frequency of directives posed as a question and voiced with intonation of a question, such as "why don't you go ahead and show me?"

Students' internal locus of causality and a sense of choice over their actions will be stimulated when a teacher implements autonomy supportive instructional behaviors and satisfies students' psychological basic needs, interests, and preferences; while students' external locus of causality, high pressure, and a sense of assignment will be generated when a teacher relies only on outer motivational resources and pressuring language with controlling instructional behaviors. The autonomy-supportive instructional behavior can be understood as student-centered instruction while controlling instructional behavior can be understood as leading students towards a teacher-defined instruction.

Teachers who teach in an autonomy-supportive motivating style facilitate students' autonomy to enhance their intrinsic motivation, which could finally improve students' learning engagement (Jang et al., 2010). He (2009) conducted non-experimental research which examined the Self-determination Theory applied in a language learning context and explored the connections between ESL students' perceived teacher's autonomy support, intrinsic motivation, and learning engagement. The study adopted the conceptual model from Patrick et al.'s (2007) study, which stated that the classroom learning environment would impact students' motivation, and motivation in turn would influence students' engagement in turn. The results showed that the more autonomy supports the students perceived, the higher their intrinsic motivation. Meanwhile, intrinsic motivation could predict students' engagement. In addition, the results also showed that perceived teacher's autonomy support was positively correlated with learning engagement, which demonstrated that the more autonomy supports the students perceived, the higher their learning engagement. Intrinsic motivation played a partial mediating effect between perceived autonomy support and the effect of learning engagement.

Alrabai (2021) conducted an empirical study that stated that EFL students with teacher's autonomy-support intervention had increased EFL autonomy. During the experiment, EFL students' perceived choice, autonomy support, intrinsic motivation mediated the relationship between teacher's autonomy supportive teaching and learners' autonomy. The results identified the vital role of teacher's autonomy support in promoting EFL students' autonomy, which would satisfy students' basic psychological needs.

By review on the previous literature related to teacher's emotional support, cognitive support, and autonomy support, different operational behaviors had been listed. In the current study, relevant teacher supportive behavior will be chosen from the previous studies. More detailed information had been organized in Table 2-6.

Table 2-6 Operational Behaviors in Three Types of Teacher Support

Strategy	Operational Behaviors	Researcher
Teacher's Emotional Support	· Paying positive attention to learners' learning status	Chai and Gong (2013) Jia (2018) Jiang et al. (2018a) Liu et al. (2017)
	· Supporting students' emotions when dealing with pressure and challenges · Thinking from students' point of view · Spending time in helping students	Chai and Gong (2013)
	· Prompt response and feedback	Jia (2018) Jiang et al. (2018a) Liu et al. (2017)
	· Providing encouragement to online learners' study · Stimulating learners' motivation and enthusiasm for learning	Liu et al. (2017)
	· Creating positive learning climate	Jiang et al. (2018a) Liu et al. (2017)
	· Expectation on learners' study · Using humorous and emotional symbols and expressions in online communication	Jiang et al. (2018a)
	· Giving praise on students' improvement and performance	Jiang et al. (2018b)
	· Participating interaction and discussion with students	Jia (2018) Jiang et al. (2018b) Liu et al. (2017)
	· Sharing teacher's point of view with students	Jia (2018)

续表

Strategy	Operational Behaviors	Researcher
Teacher's Cognitive Support	· Providing learning strategies to improve students' academic ability	Chai et al. (2011) Jia (2018) Liu et al. (2017) Richard et al. (2007)
	· Providing students with challenging but achievable tasks	Chai and Gong (2013) Chi (2017) Lam and Law (2007) Law (2011) Liu et al. (2017)
	· Stimulating learners' curiosity	Lam and Law (2007) Law (2011)
	· Connecting learning content to learners' real-life experiences	Chai and Gong (2013) Law (2011)
	· Recognizing learners' efforts in learning	Law (2011)
	· Being good at guiding students to think instead of giving answer directly · Applying simple way to explain complex concept	Chai and Gong (2013) Chi (2017) Richard et al. (2007)
	· Using multimedia resources to create a language learning environment · Providing help when students encountering difficulties in learning.	Jia (2018)
Teacher's Autonomy Support	· Accepting students' opinion and feeling	Deci and Ryan (1985) Skinner and Belmont (1993) Chai and Gong (2013)

续表

Strategy	Operational Behaviors	Researcher
Teacher's Autonomy Support	· Providing diversified resources	Chi (2017) Deci and Ryan (1985) Jia (2018) Liu et al. (2017)
	· Low controlling behavior	Chai and Gong (2013) Chi (2017) Skinner and Belmont (1993)
	· Providing appropriate opportunities for students' academic activities	Jia (2018) Liu et al. (2017) Skinner and Belmont (1993)
	· Giving students enough freedom and support in arranging academic tasks and choosing learning content	Chai and Gong (2013) Liu et al. (2017)
	· Providing opportunities to express themselves · Encouraging students to be responsible for their own learning	Chi (2017)
	· Adjusting teaching process according to students' autonomous learning	Jia (2018)

3) Studies on Teacher Support Regarding Learning Engagement, Learning Attitude, and Academic Achievement

Among the studies related to teacher support, the effectiveness of teacher support and its relation with other variables have mostly been investigated. Teacher support has been proved to have a positive influence on students' psychology, learning motivation, learning engagement and learning achievement (Dincer et al., 2012; Klem & Connell, 2004; Olani et al., 2010; Piechurska-Kuciel, 2011; Tas, 2016; Tas et al., 2019; Wentzl, 1998; Zohre et al., 2017).

(1) Studies on Teacher Support Regarding Learning Engagement

Klem and Connell (2004) viewed teacher support containing structure, autonomy support and involvement, and investigated the relationships among teacher support, learning engagement and academic achievement. The study showed that students' learning engagement was more influenced by teacher support at middle school than at elementary school. The results proved that teacher support is an important factor affecting students' learning engagement. In turn, high engagement is positively correlated with students' achievement and academic performance.

In an EFL context, Dincer et al. (2012) examined the relationship between autonomy-supportive or controlled learning climate and EFL students' learning engagement and speaking competence. In their study, it stated that teacher's autonomy supportive behaviors were positively related to EFL students' learning engagement. In addition, when students felt autonomy supported by their teachers, they had higher levels of perceived competence in speaking. Consequently, they participated in the course activities more volitionally and their course achievements were generally good. It was believed that students who perceived more autonomy support from teachers had higher levels of oral proficiency, participated more actively in classroom activities, and perform better in evaluation. Dincer and Yesilyurt (2017) investigated the relationship between university EFL learner's autonomy support, autonomous regulation, motivation to speak, and classroom engagement in Turkey. The quantitative results of the study confirmed the previous studies that students' intrinsic motivation was higher than other orientations and it was correlated with teacher's autonomy support and classroom engagement. It also concluded from the qualitative interview that although students' intrinsic motivation was the most influential motivational factor, other motivational factors (such as teacher's support) also played roles in students' volition to speak.

Tas (2016) investigated the relations between students' engagement, motivation, and classroom learning environment in which teacher support was found to be significant and consistent in predicating students' engagement. Later, Tas et al. (2019) investigated the effects of teacher support on students' motivation and engagement in science class. It was found to positively influence students' task-value, self-concept and engagement. If the teacher behaves in a predictable way, students may be more willing to learn and more engaged in their behaviors. If the teacher gives students more care and concerns, students may be more enthusiastic about the class and more emotionally engaged (Tas et al., 2019).

Students who are supported by the teacher have positive attitudes (Battistich et al., 1995), which would lead to a significant improvement in students' academic engagement (Marks, 2000; Skinner & Belmont, 1993).

(2) Studies on Teacher Support Regarding Learning Attitude

In the EFL context, a study conducted by Noels and her colleagues (1999) proposed that teacher support had a positive effect on students' intrinsic motivation when learning a foreign language. Students felt a stronger desire to learn a language and continue learning when teachers give more informative and clearer instruction to support their autonomy. Later, Noels et al. (2000) examined the relationship between students' motivation, perceived competence and language learning achievement in a bilingual university. It was found that students' increased sense of freedom of choice was more linked to intrinsic motivation in language learning and the results showed that teacher's autonomy-supportive instructional style could promote students' intrinsic motivation, sense of self-determination, and increased perceived learning outcomes.

Piechurska-Kuciel (2011) investigated the relationship between teacher support and language anxiety level in EFL students. It proved that students who received higher levels of teacher support had lower levels of language anxiety than those who received lower levels of teacher support and had higher scores in the examination. In the study, teacher support is divided into four dimensions: emotional support, instrumental support, information support and evaluative support.

Zohre et al. (2017) regarded teacher support played a vital role in improving students' performance in learning a language and investigated the relationship between teacher support, motivational orientation, English reading strategies. It was shown that students' perceived teacher support was directly and significantly correlated with students' intrinsic motivation. While no significant correlation was shown between teacher support and extrinsic motivation.

Teacher's autonomy support played an important role in improving students' motivation. In the EFL context, Yesilyurt (2008) found that students' perceived autonomy support had a significant relationship with different motivations. The results also showed that more autonomous types of motivation were stronger correlated with students' perceived autonomy support in English writing classes. By facilitating autonomy support in the EFL learning environment, it could enhance students' intrinsic motivation and accordingly, EFL students' performance in English writing.

Jin and Dewaele (2018) investigated the role of teacher emotional support in EFL learning anxiety among English major students at a public university in China. Different results were proposed that perceived teacher emotional support did not significantly predict EFL students' classroom anxiety. It was explained that teacher's emotional support under a teacher-centered environment had little effect on adult students' language anxiety. Moreover, as the age grows, students tend to pursue more mentally and behaviorally independence.

By analyzing the previous studies about teacher support, it could be found that teacher support is positively related to students' affective factors, learning engagement and learning achievements. Furthermore, Reeve (2012) proposed that teacher's support on students' autonomy is the central feature in the learning environment. It could predict students' learning engagement and learning achievement by working on students' affective factors based on the SDT framework (Jang et al., 2012). Therefore, in order to satisfy EFL students' basic needs and promote EFL students' interest and maintain persistence in learning English, it is necessary to further investigate the effect of teacher's support from different aspects.

(3) Studies on Teacher Support Regarding Academic Achievement

As one kind of personal relation, teacher support had a direct influence on students' learning interests to influence students' academic achievement (Wentzl, 1998). Olani et al. (2010) empirically tested the effects of students' perceived teacher support and self-efficacy beliefs on their learning achievement. The result showed perceived teacher support indirectly facilitates students' learning achievement. It had been proved that students with teacher's autonomy support displayed more impressive on their academic achievements than those of students with teacher's controls (Reeve et al., 2004; Reeve, 2009).

Another research on teacher's autonomy support in the EFL context was presented by O'Reilly (2014), which used a longitudinal design and examined the relationships between perceived teacher's autonomy support, intrinsic motivation, and language outcomes. Different from other studies viewing students' language ability as learning achievement, this study adopted students' Grade Point Average (GPA) of their language course. By analysis on students' intrinsic motivation and the learning climate questionnaire, the results showed that EFL students' perceived autonomy support was significantly correlated to a higher level of intrinsic motivation and moderately enhanced students' learning achievement.

In Oga-Baldwin's (2020) study, how teacher support influences EFL students' autonomy was investigated and the effects of teacher's autonomy supportive behaviors on students' attendance and achievement were explored. The result showed that students who perceived more support from their teacher had higher academic attendance and learning achievement, while those who perceived more controlling and intrusive teaching had lower attendance and achievement. What should be paid attention to in the study was that when students were required to enroll in compulsory classes, their intrinsic motivation may be less important. Meanwhile, the learning environment created by teachers tended to be more important for students' attendance and achievement.

In Sadoughi and Hejazi's study (2021), the researchers explored the effects of teacher support on EFL learners' learning engagement with the mediation of academic emotions. Teacher support was divided into three dimensions which were instrumental support, appraisal support, and emotional support. The results showed that emotional support was significantly correlated with all components of learning engagement. Additionally, teacher support was indirectly correlated to learning engagement through positive emotions. But it also showed that students did not perceive emotional support as much as instrumental support, thus it showed that teacher emotional support had less predicting effect on students' learning engagement and positive emotions than instrumental support.

Phakiti (2003) explored the relationship between providing cognitive and meta-cognitive strategy and university EFL students' reading achievement. Since meta-cognition includes active monitoring and corresponding regulation and coordination of cognitive processes to achieve cognitive goals. In order to achieve cognitive goals, teachers need to provide proper instructions and help for students' to develop their cognitive and metacognitive ability. In Phakiti's (2003) study, the results showed that students' meta-cognitive ability and cognitive ability were positively related to their reading achievement, but no significance was shown between them. While in a similar study conducted by Zare-ee (2007), it was shown that meta-cognitive ability was significantly related to EFL students' reading achievement. Both studies indicated that relevant cognitive supports provided by teachers were also positively related to students' English reading achievement.

Sarafianou and Gavriilidou (2015) investigated the effect of strategy-based instruction on secondary school EFL students' strategy use in Greek. Pre and post surveys were conducted. The results showed that students who were taught with strategies reported significant improvement in strategy use, which confirmed the 'teachability' of learning strategies and also indicated the possibility of teacher's cognitive support in strategy learning. It also suggested that "explicit and integrated strategy training should have a role in EFL classroom" (Sarafianou & Gavriilidou, 2015. p. 21). It mentioned that studies have shown that explicit strategic guidance could enable learners to understand the importance and purpose of strategy learning and provide them opportunities for practice and self-evaluation (Cohen et al., 1998; Gavriilidou & Papanis, 2009). By providing strategy-based instruction, it enables students to understand and assess the application of strategies.

Mirsane and Khabiri (2016) pointed out that because the willingness to communicate is one of the most powerful predictors of being proficient in language learning, it is necessary to provide support on teaching communicative strategy for EFL learners. In addition, teaching communicative strategy cannot be overlooked in improving students' language proficiency (Dörnyei, 1995). Therefore, they conducted an empirical study that investigated the effect of teaching communicative strategy on EFL learners' willingness to communicate, which in turn, influencing EFL students' language proficiency. The results showed that communicative strategies instruction significantly influenced EFL learners' willingness to communicate, which in turn might have a positive influence on students' language proficiency.

2. Learning Engagement

1) Definition of Learning Engagement

The concept of student learning engagement was partly generated from the Social Control Theory (Hirschi, 1969), which emphasized the social bond between individuals and the social context. There are four interrelated forms of social bond, which are: attachment, commitment, belief, and involvement. Those social bonds laid the foundation for the theory of student engagement.

In earlier research, student learning engagement appeared in the students' drop-out model to explain the process which caused students to drop out from school (Tinto, 1975). Student learning engagement, also known as student involvement, student engagement, or academic engagement, appeared in Astin's (1984) work which studied students' involvement. Astin (1984) defined it as "the amount of physical and psychological energy the student devotes to the academic experience" (p. 518). Astin (1984) developed the student involvement theory in which emphasized more on students' behavioral engagement in academic activities. Because he regarded involvement as the behavioral manifestation of students' psychological state. In the involvement theory, students become the focus of concern and it proposes that teachers should focus less on what they do and more on what students do.

Although student learning engagement is also regarded as student involvement, it is still different from involvement. Engagement requires not only activity, but also feeling and sense-making during the learning process (Harper & Quaye, 2009). Because "acting without feeling engaged is just involvement or even compliance; feeling engaged without acting is dissociation (Trowler, 2010. p. 5).

Therefore, following Astin's definition of student involvement, the concept was expanded by incorporating the earlier concept such as time-on-task (Merwin, 1969) and quality of effort (Pace, 1984) with later work concerning teaching and learning practice, generating the concept of "student engagement" (Kuh et al., 1991). Later, Hu and Kuh (2001, p. 3) defined learning engagement as the "quality of effort students themselves devote to educationally purposeful activities that contribute directly to desired outcomes". Kuh (2001a) defined learning engagement as the time and efforts that students take part in activities related to their expected academic outcomes, as well as the efforts the school makes to support students' involvement in these activities. He asserted that the more students positively engage in their course content, the more academic achievement they could obtain.

Kuh (2001a) and his colleagues developed the National Survey of Student Engagement (NSSE) to evaluate the extent that university students were engaged in their school learning and what they gained from their school experience. With the popularity and application of the NSSE survey, student engagement has been widely researched. The results from the NSSE project have been applied to establish a series of national standards on effective teaching and participating schools have used it to evaluate the effects of their improvement efforts (Kuh, 2001b). Results from the NSSE project showed that students' learning achievement was positively correlated with their engagement. Meanwhile, high-level engagement and high-level achievements could promote each other (Kuh, 2001a). As the NSSE survey entered the research field of other countries, Tsinghua University in China introduced the NSSE survey project into China and improved it into NSSE-China according to the characteristics of Chinese university students. In 2009, it was evolved into the China College Student Survey (CCSS), which has formed a kind of student-centered research tool that focuses on the learning process and examines students' learning and future development (CCSS, 2009).

The definitions above mostly view learning engagement from the perspective of behavior. There are also some studies exploring learning engagement from the perspective of motivation and psychology. For example, Lam et al. (2014) proposed that student engagement is a psychological process and a mediating variable between learning context and learning achievement, which is reflected by the students' effort, interest and involvement.

Considering the multifaceted feature of student engagement, some scholars regard learning engagement should be a multidimensional construct (Fredricks et al., 2004; Skinner et al., 1990). Skinner et al. (1990) view learning engagement as including behavioral and emotional engagement and define it as containing students' initiation of action, effort, persistence on school tasks, and emotional states during learning. In a study conducted by Klem and Connell (2004), student reports of learning engagement showed that the proportion of students who were not engaged in school increased from elementary to middle and high schools. In contrast, teacher reports of learning engagement showed oppositely that fewer students were disengaging from elementary to middle school. The difference between students' and teachers' reports on their perception of learning engagement might be due to the different measurements in two groups' reports, in which students' reports were observed from their emotional and behavioral aspects while teacher's reports observed only from students' behavioral aspect.

Fredricks et al. (2004) regard that learning engagement is influenced by the context or environment and it will be changed respectively according to the environment. With the multifaceted feature, Fredricks et al. (2004) proposed that learning engagement is a multidimensional concept that contains behavioral engagement, emotional engagement and cognitive engagement in a comprehensive and meaningful way. Integration of the three types of engagement is valuable because it provides a richer description of learners than which is in the research on single components. The three kinds of learning engagement are not independently separated, but dynamically interrelated.

Others have defined learning engagement as a positive and fulfilling mental state associated with learning and it is a comprehensive response of students' efforts, teachers' requirements and school support (Yang & Han, 2013). According to Trowler (2010), learning engagement "is concerned with the interaction between the time, effort and other relevant resources invested by both students and their institutions to optimize students' experience and enhance the learning outcomes and development of students and the performance, and reputation of the institution" (p. 2).

2) *Classification of Learning Engagement*

Because the definition of learning engagement may vary slightly in different contexts (Fredricks et al., 2004), there have been different classifications and dimensions of learning engagement. Some scholars view learning engagement as a two-dimensional model. In Finn's (1989) study, students' learning engagement was classified into behavioral engagement and emotional engagement. Behavioral engagement refers to students' involvement in classroom and school activities, while emotional engagement refers to students' identification with school, which is a kind of belonging.

Connell and Wellborn (1994) and Skinner (1995) defined and divided two forms of engagement: one is ongoing engagement and another is the reaction to challenge. In his ongoing engagement, which is similar to other definitions of engagement and refers to students' emotional, behavioral engagement as well as the thought processes during the school day. Behavioral engagement includes the intensity of effort and concentration on the study, time students spent on study, tendency to stay on task, inclination to carry out an action when an opportunity is given. Emotional engagement means positive emotional status when completing an activity, which might be in an enthusiastic, optimistic, curious and interested status. Another engagement in their study is the reaction to challenge, which refers to an optimistic attitude or attempts to prevent problems from occurring in the future by using strategies to cope with challenges. If students are threatened by a problem situation and perceive failure from it, they might avoid such activity when encountered in the future (Connell & Wellborn, 1994; Skinner 1995).

Skinner et al. (2008) regard that high quality learning is the outcome of behavior and emotion. Therefore, behavioral engagement and emotional engagement combine the two-dimension model of student engagement. "The behavioral dimension of engagement includes students' effort, attention, and persistence during the initiation and execution of learning activities. The emotional dimension of engagement focuses on states that are germane to students' emotional involvement during learning activities such as enthusiasm, interest, and enjoyment" (p. 766).

As shown in Table 2-7, different dimensions of students' learning engagement are presented. Other studies have proposed a three-dimension model of learning engagement that usually includes behavioral, cognitive and emotional engagement (Fredricks et al., 2004; Jimerson et al., 2003; Wigfield et al., 2008). The current study adopted the three-dimension construct of learning engagement from Fredricks et al. (2004), which is one of the most prevalent divisions for engagement.

Table 2-7 Classifications of Student Learning Engagement

	Dimension of Learning Engagement	Researcher
Two Dimensions	· behavioral engagement · emotional engagement	Finn (1989); Skinner (2008)
	· ongoing engagement · reaction to challenge	Connell and Wellborn (1994) Skinner (1995)
Three Dimensions	· behavioral engagement · cognitive engagement · emotional engagement	Fredricks et al. ,(2004) Jimmersion(2003) Wigfield et al. (2008) Ma et al. (2019)
	· cognitive engagement · social engagement · emotional engagement	Svalberg (2009)
Four Dimensions	· behavioral engagement · cognitive engagement · emotional engagement · social engagement	Luan et al. (2020) Philp andDuchesue (2016) Rimm-Kaufman (2015)
	· behavioral engagement · cognitive engagement · academic engagement · psychological engagement	Appleton et al. (2006)

Drawing on Bloom (1956), Fredricks et al. (2004) viewed learning engagement as a three-multifaceted construct and defined them separately in terms of behavioral engagement, emotional engagement and cognitive engagement. Behavioral engagement refers to the positive behaviors in following classroom rules and norms, engaging in learning and academic tasks, in participation in school-related activities. It means students' involvement in academic, or social activities.

It is regarded as the key component to positive learning achievement and dropout prevention(Connell & Wellborn ,1991).

As to cognitive engagement, it contains "being thoughtful, strategic, willing to exert effort for comprehension of complex ideas or mastery of difficult skills". (Fredricks et al. ,2012. p. 764). It refers to the inner psychological investment and quality in learning, a desire to go beyond the requirements, and a preference for a challenge. It also refers to the state of being strategic and or self-regulating. It is believed that if scholars combine the specificity of cognitive processes in self-regulated theory with definitions of psychological investment in motivational theory, the idea of cognitive engagement would be more valuable(Fredricks et al. ,2004).

Emotional engagement refers to students' affective reactions in the classroom. It focuses on students' positive or negative emotions toward their teachers, classmates, or school. It is students' identification with the school, which would influence students' satisfaction in their basic psychological needs (Finn, 1989). Some research viewed students' emotional engagement as their identification with school, which is a kind of belonging (Finn, 1989). It overlaps with the part of belonging in motivational research. Especially, belonging is one of the basic needs in Self-Determination Theory (Deci & Ryan, 2000). This three-dimension model of learning engagement has been widely acknowledged and used in different studies about student engagement. For instance, Wang and Eccles (2013), Hospel and Galand (2016) all applied Fredricks' three-dimension model of engagement in their empirical studies.

However, with the application of information technology in education, there has not been much work focusing on student engagement in the blended learning environment (Ma et al., 2019). Ma et al. (2017) conducted an initial development of students engagement scale in a blended learning environment based on Fredricks et al.'s (2004) three dimensions of student engagement. Based on the initial studies, she further investigated the engagement of Chinese students in a blended learning environment. By theoretical review and empirical analysis, the three dimensions of students' engagement were further refined into six factors, which areactive learning, teacher-student interaction, and group work under behavioral engagement, implementing learning strategy and self-regulation under cognitive engagement, and emotional involvement under emotional engagement (Ma et al., 2019).

Considering the features of engagement in foreign language learning, although the importance of social interactive engagement has been emphasized (Philp and Duchesne, 2016), teacher-student interaction and group work in behavioral engagement have already manifested the feature of social interactive characteristics in foreign language learning. What's more, Ma et al.'s (2017; 2019) three-dimension engagement was proposed under the Chinese blended learning context, which has considered the Chinese educational and social background.

Therefore, the current study takes the point of three-dimension learning engagement raised by Fredricks et al. (2004) and improved by Ma et al. (2019). From this point of view, students' learning engagement can be studied from a more comprehensive perspective. Different from the two-dimension construct which only contains behavioral and emotional engagement, the three-dimension engagement enlarges its contents of cognitive engagement, which takes into account students' cognitive process (Ma et al., 2019). Integration of behavioral engagement, emotional engagement and cognitive engagement is valuable because it provides a richer description of learners than which is in research on single components (Fredricks et al., 2004).

There have also been some conceptualized learning engagement as a four-dimension model or even a model with more than four components. For example, based on Fredricks et al.'s (2004) study, Rimm-Kaufman (2015) added social engagementto the three dimensions. Appleton et al. (2006) viewed student engagement as academic, behavioral, cognitive and psychological engagement. Academic engagement can be manifested as time spent on task, academic credits earned and completion on their assignment; behavioral engagement here performs as participation in classroom and extra-curriculum activities; cognitive engagement could be performed as self-regulation, learning values, and correlation between the curriculum tasks and future effort; psychological engagement could be manifested as identification, belonging and teacher-student relationship, etc. Luan et al. (2020) viewed student engagement as behavioral, emotional, cognitive and social engagement.

Under the EFL context, Svalberg (2009) pointed out the concept of Engagement with the Language (EWL), which consists of cognitive engagement, social engagement, and emotional engagement. With further studies of engagement in language learning, Philp and Duchesne (2016) proposed a more comprehensive model ofstudents engagement, which defines engagement as a kind of status with a high degree of attention and involvement. Under this status, students' participation is manifested not only through behavioral, emotional, and cognitive aspects but also through social aspects. Both Svalberg (2009) and Philp (2016) regarded the social dimension to interaction should be emphasized as a dimension of engagement. Therefore, learning engagement under a language learning environment is a multi-dimension concept with behavioral engagement, emotional engagement, cognitive engagement, and social engagement (Philp & Duchesne, 2016). Compared with the three-dimension engagement in psychological education, this definition emphasized the interactive social dimension under the language teaching and learning context. In the field of EFL teaching, this four-dimensional engagement is regarded as a comprehensive conceptual framework of students engagement (Xu & Fan, 2019).

Based on Kuh's definition of learning engagement, whether students positively engaged in learning activities could be mainly identified from five benchmarks: 1) "students' active and collaborative learning, 2) participation in challenging academic activities, 3) formative communication with academic staff, 4) involvement in enriching educational experiences, and 5) feeling legitimated and supported by university learning communities" (Trowler, 2010. p. 7). These elements comprised the basis of the National Survey of Students Engagement.

It could be found that student learning engagement is a multidimensional concept and it can be varied and changed according to different contexts (Fredricks et al., 2004). Even with the same conceptualized dimensions, it could be different in the specific item when measured by different instruments (Fredricks et al., 2012). Although the concept of each dimension is different from each other, they are not independent and exclusive to each other (Chi,2017). For example, when students have higher engagement on one dimension, other dimensions of engagement will be relatively changed (Sinatra et al. ,2015).

3) Studies on Learning Engagement in Educational Context

The factors that might influence students' learning engagement can be mainly classified into individual factors and external environment factors (Fredricks et al. ,2004). Personal factors refer to the factors that come from an individual's personal psychological or behavioral factors. While external environment factors refer to the factors which come from teachers, peers, family, and the learning environment (Hu et al. ,2019). However, the external factors of student behavior and peers and family are beyond the scope of this study. Here, we focus on the influence of students' psychology, teacher, and learning environment on student engagement.

Klem and Connell (2004) estimated the threshold levels of engagement affect students' performance. Students' learning engagement is strongly associated with students' achievement. In elementary and middle school, students who engaged at a high level were more likely to perform well on their achievement and attendance.

Wang and Eccles (2013) investigated the relationship between students' perception of the school environment, achievement motivation and student engagement. The results showed that different aspects of students' perception of the school environment could influence students' achievement motivation and thus influence the three types of students engagement. Jung and Lee (2018) investigated how to facilitate students' learning engagement in a Massive Open Online Course

(MOOC). It was found that perceived self-efficacy, teaching presence, and perceived usefulness had a direct and positive influence on students' learning engagement.

Vaughan (2014) investigated the influence of collaborative learning application in a blended learning environment on student engagement to promote students' course achievement and satisfaction. It demonstrated that there was a moderate to strong correlations between the use of digital technology and student engagement in a blended learning environment.

(1) Studies on Learning Engagement in the EFL Context

In the EFL context, Sahin-kizil (2014) designed a blended language course based on Moodle in the EFL context and explored the effect of blended design on students' learning engagement and overall course satisfaction. It proposed that technology-assisted language instruction could provide paralleled supplement with face-to-face instruction to create an effective learning environment in which students could more engage in language learning. The results showed that most students agreed that the use of Moodle increased their engagement in the course and expressed satisfaction on their engagement.

Student engagement in learning has been proven to positively influence students' language achievement. For example, the study of Alsowat (2016) investigated the effect of an EFL flipped classroom teaching model on university students' thinking skills, engagement and satisfaction and also examined the relationships between them. The findings showed that before and after the flipped teaching model was applied, students' engagement increased significantly. Moreover, there was a significant relationship between students' engagement and satisfaction.

Based on the Self-Determination Theory and Self-System model of motivation, Huang et al. (2017) applied collaborative digital storytelling in an EFL language course, which lasted 17 months and explored the students' pair performance, flow perception concerning their language proficiency level. EFL students' language proficiency level was found to be an influencing factor of their engagement and pair performance.

Fisher et al. (2018) conducted an empirical study to explore the relationship between flipped and blended learning instruction and students' engagement outcomes. It was found that flipped and blended learning positively influenced students' perceptions of engagement, performance and satisfaction. But flipped learning mediated the effect of blended learning on students' performance. Meanwhile, the engagement stimulated by flipped learning satisfied students' perceptions of independent performance, which consequently led to students' satisfaction.

Jung and Lee (2018) investigated how to facilitate students' learning engagement and persistence in a Massive Open Online Course (MOOC). It was found that perceived self-efficacy, teaching presence, and perceived usefulness had a direct and positive influence on students' learning engagement. In addition, teaching presence and perceived ease of use had a direct influence on students' learning persistence.

Ahmad (2019) conducted an empirical study that applied digital posters in an EFL reading course. The effect of digital posters on EFL students' reading comprehension and engagement was discussed. The findings showed that there were significant differences in students' reading proficiency between the control and experimental groups in the post-reading test. It showed that student engagement could be improved by developing students' digital literacy skills and students' reading comprehension could be enhanced when engagement increased.

Ghanizadeh et al. (2020) investigated the relationship between the corrective feedback teaching model, EFL students' engagement, motivation and language achievement by quantitative and qualitative methods. The result revealed that students' behavioral, emotional, and cognitive engagement were all influenced by the teaching method in the experimental group and emotional engagement performed the highest difference and behavioral engagement performed the lowest difference. And the experimental group demonstrated higher language achievement under the influence of the corrective feedback teaching model.

(2) Studies on Learning Engagement and Teacher Support

Students' psychological and behavioral factors are the main personal factors that could influence their engagement. Since teachers play a vital role in classroom learning. They pass on the knowledge to students based on the instructional theories and professional knowledge they have mastered (Chi, 2017). Teacher's teaching methods and teaching models are the key factors influencing students' learning (Hu et al., 2019).

To enhance students' online learning motivation and engagement, autonomy support was applied as a strategy and three guidelines were proposed as the core of the strategy for educators and course designers (Lee et al. ,2015). In Skinner et al. 's (2008) study, teacher support and students' perceived autonomy were positively related to behavioral engagement. Students' perception of teacher support played a mediated role between teacher support and students' engagement, especially behavioral engagement.

Ryan and Patrick (2001) explored the influence of perceived teacher support, peer interactive encouragement on students learning motivation, and learning engagement. It showed that perceived teacher support and peer's interactive encouragement were positively correlated to students' learning motivation and learning engagement.

Ferrell (2012) investigated the influence of learning environment including teacher support and peer support and motivation on students' behavioral, emotional, and cognitive engagement. It was found that teacher support and peer support could positively predicate students' motivation. In addition, it showed that learning objective was significantly correlated to the three types of engagement while self-efficacy only significantly correlated to cognitive engagement.

Dincer et al. (2012) investigated the effect of teacher support on EFL students' engagement and English speaking ability by creating an autonomy-supportive learning environment in the classroom. It was proved that students who felt autonomy support from their teacher had a higher perception of their English speaking competence. Those who felt competent in speaking willingly participated in classroom activities. In brief, teacher's autonomy supportive behaviors were positively and significantly correlated with students' engagement and their achievements. Later, Dincer et al. (2019) investigated the outcomes of Turkish EFL student engagement. It examined the relationships between perceived teacher's autonomy support, students' psychological needs, engagement, and language learning outcome. The study reported that student engagement could predict their achievement within an English class and engagement could be predicted by their need satisfaction when the teacher's autonomy support was perceived. In addition, semi-structured interviews with EFL students emphasized that language teachers played a vital role in supporting students' psychological need satisfaction, learning engagement, and language outcomes.

Tas et al. (2019) investigated the relationship between teacher's support and learning engagement and analyzed the relationship among the three types of learning engagement. The result shows that other engagement will increase if one aspect of engagement increased. In addition, since teacher's teaching style has an important impact on students' engagement, Jiang and Zhang (2021) divided teacher's teaching style into perceived autonomy support, social relatedness and controlling and investigated the relationship of the three types of teaching style to university students' agentic engagement in EFL learning in China. The agentic engagement in the study refers to "students' constructive contribution into the flow of the instruction they receive" (Reeve & Tseng, 2011. p. 258). The results showed that perceived autonomy support teaching style positively predicted students' agentic engagement, whereas perceived controlling teaching style negatively predicted students' agentic engagement.

Considering the results of the previous literature, it could be found that teacher behaviors, teacher support and learning environment can not only directly affect students' learning engagement, but also indirectly affect students' learning engagement through mediating variables such as motivation (Chi, 2017). The majority of studies on learning engagement have been related to students' learning improvement or outcomes (Trowler, 2010). The ultimate goal for studying students' learning engagement was to improve students' learning outcomes (Pascarella et al., 2010). A great deal of literature has proven that student' learning engagement has been positively influenced by teacher support (Ryan & Patrick, 2001; Tas et al., 2019) and been significantly related to students' achievement and competence (Connell, 1991; 1994; Kim D, 1995) but also positively predicate on students' learning development (such as satisfaction, persistence) (Astin, 1984; Kuh et al. 2005). However, it can be found that few studies explored the influence of teacher support on EFL students' learning engagement under a blended learning environment. In the current study, there is a need to further investigate the effect of teacher support on students' learning engagement in a blended learning environment.

3. Language Learning Attitude

According to the Oxford dictionary, attitude refers to the way one thinks and feels about somebody or something and the way one behaves towards somebody or something that shows how one thinks and feels. Hanula (2002) stated that emotions aroused in a situation, and emotions associated with a stimulus in study can be identified as the term of learning attitude. Moreover, language learning attitude is closely related to language learning (Starks &Paltridge, 1996), and there have been studies confirmed that learners' language learning attitude is one of the most critical factors in determining the success of language learning (Ehrman et al. 2003).

It is believed that a good language learner is one who knows how to control their academic emotions and learning attitude because a positive language learning attitude could make language learning more effective and interesting (Kimura, 2000). Zhang and Yuan (2004) once pointed out that learners' self-confidence and learning anxiety are the two important emotional factors in learning attitude. For example, Truitt (1995) found that Korean EFL students with high level of language anxiety admitted more difficulties in learning English and felt less self-confidence when speaking English. Kitano (2001) also stated that when students have lower levels of self-confidence, they may generate stronger feelings of language anxiety. Similarly, MacIntyre et al. (1997) found that students who are prone to be anxious in the language classroom are more likely to be diffident in their language proficiency, which may lead to discrepancies between their self-perceptions and their actual language performance. Therefore, to avoid this situation, language teachers need to make greater efforts and provide appropriate support to increase students' self-confidence in their language proficiency and reduce students' language anxiety to help them achieve better academic goals (Liu & Chen, 2013).

Previous studies showed that self-confidence and language anxiety as elements of language learning attitudes have become important factors affecting the effectiveness of learners' language learning. Foreign language learning involves many cultural and psycho-social factors which would also influence learners' attitudes in different ways. Learners may relate their beliefs, experiences, and emotions to language learning which are directly or indirectly influenced by the classroom environment. Teacher support, teacher-student relationships, classroom learning activities, and classroom collaboration constitute the classroom learning dimension.

According to the Self-Determination Theory, when the basic needs of individuals are satisfied, their intrinsic motivation will be stimulated (Deci & Ryan, 2000). Teacher support, had been also confirmed its function in stimulating students' learning motivation and it could be regarded as one trigger of students' learning motivation. Once the motivation is confirmed, learners usually take a positive learning attitude to achieve their goals. Therefore, students' learning attitudes, especially students' self-confidence and language anxiety, were involved in the current study to explore the effects of teacher support on EFL students' language learning attitude.

1) Self-Confidence in the EFL Context

According to Ansari and Oskrochi (2004), self-confidence is related to selection, motivation, perseverance, vulnerability, patterns of subjective expectations, ambition, and ambitious influence of one's self. Therefore, a person with high self-confidence is more likely to achieve positive and successful outcomes. A similar opinion is stated by Adalikwu (2012) that self-confidence is a belief that someone has it in his/her ability to succeed in a task, based on whether he/she is able to do that task or not in the past. So, when students are confident about their abilities irrespective of their past experiences, they will succeed in their learning. Lawrence (2006) states that self-confidence is a set of beliefs about one's talents and abilities. Thus, confident students are successful in their learning because they believe in their abilities and never give up.

Under the EFL context, Clement et al. (1986) put self-confidence and language anxiety together to discuss their importance in foreign language learning. Clement (1986) argued that attitude factors were an important basis for foreign language learning. And he also believed that self-confidence is the most determinant factor of attitude and effort toward foreign language learning.

Krashen (1982) believed that learners' personality factors play an important role and influence the effectiveness of learning in second language acquisition. Learning self-confidence is of particular importance because the degree of self-confidence plays an important role in the process of language acquisition in people's subconscious. The higher the degree of self-confidence of language learners, the more positive motivation they might have.

After Krashen's affective factors, Arnold (2004) stressed the importance of learning self-confidence and mentioned that without a certain level of self-confidence, it will be difficult to achieve success by emotionally or cognitively efforts. That is, in the process of language acquisition, students with strong self-confidence are more likely to obtain the language input and language internalization. They are more actively inclined to seize opportunities, use target language to communicate actively, dare to take risks, learn from mistakes, obtain the best input and output in quantity and quality, and be brave enough to face problems. The improvement of language proficiency will promote the effect of language learning, which consequently promotes the constant growth of self-confidence, and in turn produce a positive learning circle.

Language self-confidence will also affect the language anxiety level of language learners. Learners with low self-confidence will be afraid of making mistakes and unwilling to use the target language for communication, show high levels of language anxiety, miss opportunity of the practice and application, and finally hindering the input and internalization of language, which is not conducive to the consolidation and development of language learning effect. Therefore, in English teaching, improving students' learning self-confidence can promote their learning motivation, learning engagement, and learning effects. Self-confidence is regarded as a significant factor that could influence foreign language students' performance. Students who lack confidence are usually found to be extremely fearful and timid, reluctant to express their opinions, and even unable to speak a complete meaningful sentence in English in class (Ni, 2012).

2) *Language Anxiety in the EFL Context*

Different from self-confidence, anxiety is a negative psychological state. It refers to the sense of threat caused by the individual's failure to achieve the expected goal or to overcome the immediate difficulties. The results of Gardner et al.'s (1981) study showed that language anxiety is negatively related to the quantity and quality of language acquisition. That is, the lower the level of language anxiety, the greater the quantity and quality of language acquisition, and vice versa.

According to Krashen (1982), reasons for learners' language anxiety can be summarized as follows: language learners believe that their lack of ability seriously hinders the use of target language when they need to use the target language to communicate; learner's nervousness hinders their language expression; language learners dare not use the target language to communicate because of past frustrating experiences. He also pointed out that language anxiety is not only related to the evaluation of learners' own language ability but also related to the quantity and quality of language acquisition.

Krashen (1982) believes that language anxiety greatly determines the success or failure of language acquisition in language teaching. Therefore, in classroom teaching, language teachers should take positive and effective measures or supports to minimize learners' language anxiety. For example, they may give learners a positive evaluation on their learning achievements, encourage and praise their performance more, which can ensure that the language learning environment is full of trust, enable students to learn in a relaxed language environment, and let them input and internalize language knowledge best.

In the EFL context, although self-confidence was related to communication, it was still suggested that anxiety and self-perception of language competence may also be determinants of foreign language achievement even the opportunity of using a foreign language tocommunicate with native speakers is rare (Clement, 1986). Foreign language anxiety is conceived of as "the feeling of tension and apprehension specifically associated with second language context, including speaking, listening, and learning" (MacIntyre & Gardner, 1994, p. 284). This multifaceted feeling is regarded as the affective factor that frequently impedes the learning process (Arnold & Brown, 1999). Horwitz et al. (1986) pointed out that certain types of classroom activities may increase learners' language anxiety, especially for those who were exposed to negative evaluations from their teachers or peers.

Foreign language anxiety has been described as facilitating anxiety and debilitating anxiety (Scovel, 1978), in which debilitating anxiety has negative effects on performance, facilitating anxiety is like promoting learners' performance. To pave the way for more straightforward research on the multidimensional concept, Horwitz et al. (1986) proposed foreign language anxiety. It includes three components, which are communication apprehension, test anxiety, and fear of negative evaluation. Communication apprehension refers to fears or anxiety in communicating with others; test anxiety is related to the fear of what is perceived as failure in test performance; while fear of negative evaluation means the anxiety originating from various appraisal situations. But Horwitz et al. (1986) did not view foreign language anxiety as simply a transfer of these anxieties to the foreign language classroom. It is more than a "distinct complex of self-perceptions, beliefs, feelings, and behaviors arising from the uniqueness of the language learning process" (p. 128). Since then, the uniqueness of the second or foreign language learning process has prospected, and language anxiety has been conceptually separated from other anxiety triggers (MacIntyre & Gardner, 1989).

It had been pointed out that due to the limited chance of exposure to English and native speaker, opportunities for many Asian students to practice their foreign language skills can only be realized in the classroom (Liu & Chen, 2013). University students reported that it was prevalent to feel anxious in English language learning (Liu, 2010).

3) *Studies on Language Learning Attitude in the EFL Context*

(1) Studies on Self-confidence in the EFL Context

According to Ni (2012), he viewed self-confidence as a factor in affective factors and explored its effect on English-major students in EFL teaching. The results showed that the affective factors decide the proportion of language learners' input and intake. The excellent students usually have high motivation, high self-confidence and low anxiety, and they receive and take in plenty of language input. It is a pity that there are still some students who learn a language with low motivation, low self-confidence and high anxiety, to whow teachers should give correct guidance on their affective factors.

Ghanbarpour (2016) had put anxiety and self-confidence together in a quantitative study to examine the effects of EFL learners' language self-confidence in their proficiency and language anxiety on their willingness to communicate level. The results showed that language learning self-confidence could significantly predict EFL students' willingness to communicate. Similarly, Yu and Shen (2012) investigated the predicting effects of language self-confidence in an EFL context and foreign language proficiency on the cross-cultural adaptation of Mainland Chinese international students in Australia. Results showed that students' self-confidence in a foreign language was particularly important and their foreign language proficiency and integrative motivation were additionally important for both social-cultural and academic adaptation for Mainland Chinese international students.

(2) Studies on Language Anxiety in the EFL Context

Listening anxiety was targeted in Vogely's (1998) qualitative study, where she investigated the sources of and solutions to listening anxiety and discussed pedagogical implications. Elkhafaifi (2005) suggests that foreign language learning anxiety and listening anxiety are separate but related; both negatively affect achievement. Saito et al. (1999) established that reading in a foreign language can also provoke anxiety, Sellers (2000) discovered that reading anxiety in a foreign language affects recall of passage content. Concerning writing, Cheng et al. (1999) examined the connections between second language classroom anxiety and second language writing anxiety and how these related to L2 speaking and writing achievement. Cheng (2002) further investigated students' perceptions of their writing anxiety and how it interacted with other forms of language anxiety.

Papi (2010) studied on the initiative to test a theoretical model that subsumes the ideal foreign language self, the ought-to foreign language self, and the foreign language learning experience in Dörnyei's (2009) foreign language motivational self-system, as well as English anxiety and intended effort to learn English. It was found that all variables significantly contributed to intended effort; however, while the ideal foreign language self and the foreign language learning experience decreased students' English anxiety, the ought-to foreign language self significantly made them more anxious.

However, language self-confidence and language learning anxiety have not always been studied separately. It can be known that researchers have studied them together with learning motivation in terms of affective factors. However, in recent years, there have also been some other studies that focus only on the two factors in it. For example, Tridinanti (2018) explored the correlation between EFL students' language anxiety, self-confidence, and speaking achievement of university EFL students. In that study, language anxiety and self-confidence were listed together as variables to language proficiency. The results showed that there was no significant correlation between language anxiety and EFL students' speaking proficiency. While self-confidence was significantly correlated with speech achievement. In other words, confident students have higher grades. The present study combined the learning self-confidence and language learning anxiety in Krashen's affective filter hypothesis with intrinsic motivation in Self-Determination Theory. It explored the psychological influence of teacher support on EFL students' learning attitudes.

4. Listening Proficiency

1) Listening Proficiency in EFL Context

Foreign language proficiency refers to the knowledge and abilities to use another language to do listening, speaking, reading and writing in a situation (Yamashita, 2002). Listening comprehension is a process that people constantly construct meaning during their interaction and it is a complex process that needs to deal with multilevel information from speeches (Cheng, 2011). When learning a language, "language proficiency is the ultimate goal of all language learning" (Nisbet et al., 2005, p. 101). As second language acquisition greatly depends on listening (Cook,1996) and listening is a channel for comprehension input (Krashen,1985), it is necessary to improve learners' foreign language listening proficiency.

Moreover, listening comprehension is a complex process with cognitive and affective difficulties (Yeldham,2016), students spend more than 50% of their time listening while learning a foreign language (Nunan,1998). No matter in or out of the classroom, listening is used more than other forms of communication in daily communication (Gilakjani & Ahmadi,2011) and it is given that listening proficiency is considered the foundation of effective communication in the EFL context (Deng,2015). But "due to the fact that universities pay more attention to English grammar, reading and vocabulary, EFL learners have limited listening proficiency" (Gilakjani & Ahmadi,2011. p. 978). Therefore, one purpose of the present study is to investigate the improvement of Chinese EFL students' listening proficiency. In order to examine Chinese university EFL students' language proficiency, Yan and Gu (2020) investigated Chinese EFL students' language proficiency based on the Common European Framework of Reference for Language (CEFR): learning, teaching, assessment, which stated that Chinese university EFL students' listening proficiency level was lower than their other language proficiency level when they were freshmen and sophomores.

As part of Chinese EFL Learners, students majoring in English have more chances to apply English in school, but their listening proficiency is still lower than other language proficiency (Zou et al., 2012). The actual language proficiency situation of Chinese English major students is that students' overall ability to apply English is weak and their level is not high enough (Pan & Zou, 2020). By analyzing the academic performance of English major students with the Test for English Major Level 4 and Level 8 (which are officially acknowledged as professional tests for English-major students in China), it was pointed out that English major students performed well in writing, vocabulary and grammar while weak in listening at the first two years during their university (Zou et al., 2012).

2) *Studies on Listening Proficiency in the EFL Context*

As language proficiency could be viewed as students' learning achievement, it can be influenced by many personal and/or environmental factors (Gradman & Hanania, 1991; Phon, 2017; Wang et al., 2019). For example, students' learning motivation, learning anxiety, and self-confidence can influence students' academic achievement (Asakereh & Yousofi, 2018; Gan, 2020; Luan et al., 2020; Piechurska-Kuciel, 2011). In particular, learning engagement and support from teachers, parents and peers are also the factors which may influence language proficiency (Luan et al., 2020).

Graham (2011) believed EFL learners' self-confidence and sense of control are crucial to develop their listening proficiency by effective instruction strategies implementation. Tabrizi and Saeidi (2015) found a positive correlation among EFL learners' autonomy, self-confidence and listening comprehension ability, which emphasized the importance to build learners' autonomy and self-confidence to ensure the improvement of EFL learners' listening proficiency. In addition, Harputlu and Ceylan (2014) also emphasized motivation and metacognitive strategy are two important personal factors influencing second language acquisition, and proved the significant correlation between extrinsic orientation to motivation and listening proficiency. Interestingly, the participants in the study were all from the English language teaching department, it presumed to have a more significant and high correlation between intrinsic motivation and listening proficiency, but the result only showed the significant relationship between extrinsic motivation and listening proficiency.

Among the external factors, teaching model is regarded as a key factor to influence students' listening proficiency as well. Grgurovic (2011) used commercial learning management system to combine face-to-face classroom learning with online learning based on Neumeier's (2005) course design parameters, and studied the effect of integration of the two modes in a speaking and listening course. It was found that the model could successfully integrate two modes and distributed learning content. The learning materials in the online learning were designed based on the structure of the textbook used in the classroom. And the use of LMS allowed the four language skills could be practiced in both modes. And it also showed that teacher's presence and support given to students in the blended learning model allowed for more individualized instruction than in a conventional classroom. The study also believed that adding online teaching to traditional teaching could improve students' language learning process.

Ahmad (2016) developed a flipped classroom model with a one-group pre-posttest quasi-experimental design and found its significant effect on students' listening proficiency. The flipped classroom was designed to have three phases: planning, implementation, and evaluation. After the treatment, the result of the posttest showed that students gained significant improvement in their listening proficiency. In addition, Banditvilai (2016) adopted blended learning to enhance the autonomy and language skills of university students. In the study, an e-learning lesson was developed in parallel with the conventional face-to-face language classroom. It was found that online practice in the e-learning lesson was directly beneficial to enhance students' four language skills as well as learning motivation and learning autonomy.

Regarding the external factors influencing listening proficiency, different teaching strategies, technical tools or applications have been applied into listening teaching and learning to enhance learners' listening proficiency. Abdulrahman et al(2018) conducted an empirical study using podcasts to improve high school students' listening proficiency and it was proved to be significantly effective in improving students' listening comprehension. The students also had a positive attitude in applying podcasts in a listening classroom. Moreover, Kim (2018) applied chatbot in EFL teaching and investigated its positive effects on Korean university students' listening skills. Students' listening proficiency level gained improvement from intermediate to advance level after engaging in the chatbots project.

Under the Chinese EFL context, scholars and teachers have also conducted various studies on students' listening proficiency. For example, Chang and Read (2006) did a classroom-based experiment and investigated the effects of four types of listening support, which showed that providing background knowledge about the topic is the most effective type of instructional support. Later, the effects of different types of listening support were explored among low-level English proficiency EFL learners (Chang & Read, 2007).

Zou (2013) explored the ways of students interact with teacher in a computer-assisted language learning environment and discussed how teachers provided support to help EFL students improve their listening skills using a CALL program. During the study, teachers offered student-teacher interaction and teacher's direction on students' speaking and listening skills. For example, giving feedback to students on computer listening and speaking tasks, answering students' questions whenever they had problems in their language learning. The survey showed that students preferred to obtain feedback on computer-based tasks more from their tutor, providing activities to direct students in completing tasks in class. The findings revealed that various means of teacher support motivate and help students to engage in CALL tasks effectively and students believed that teacher support helps them improve their listening and speaking skills more than they complete the task alone.

In addition, Cui (2014) developed a technology-facilitated blended learning model to improve students listening and speaking ability. Over a two-year experimental study, the results showed that students' listening and speaking skills did improve by applying a blended learning approach and students' initiative and autonomy could also be enhanced. Moreover, Huang's study (2016) stated that students felt online learning is more advantageous to listening and face-to-face learning could help learners improve interest in learning English.

From the above studies related to English listening proficiency improvement, it is easy to find that teacher's instructional strategies, teaching models and the other external factors may all be the influencing factors impacting students' listening proficiency (Graham, 2011;

Kim, 2018; Zou, 2013). Although there have been some studies focusing on the effect of teacher support on EFL students' speaking proficiency or reading proficiency (Dincer et al., 2019; Kazemi et al., 2016), there is still little research on the effect of teacher support in the area of English listening proficiency. Therefore, in the present study, it is necessary to consider the above facts and to make a further study to investigate the effects of teacher support on the development of Chinese EFL students' listening proficiency.

5. Blended Learning

1) Definition of Blended Learning

Blended learning is not a new concept. What makes it new is the adding of technology-based activities into the teaching and learning process (Zhang, 2009). Those technologies have provided opportunities for students to access more learning materials, communicate and interact with classmates, teachers and experts, and present their works inside and outside the classroom within a more available time (Zhang, 2009). Various research has been studied on blended learning and different forms of technology have been blended into the teaching or learning process, which makes it difficult to give a single definition of blended learning (Graham, 2006).

Some scholars have attempted to define blended learning by quantifying the amount of online learning activities (Allen & Seaman, 2006). For example, if a course has no content delivered online is regarded as a traditional course, if it has 1-29% web-facilitated course,

30-49% is viewed as a blended course, and one is over 80% regarded as fully online. However, other researchers have stated that seat time should be eliminated in a blended course and quantifying blended time is oversimplified (Dziuban et al., 2006). According to Singh and Reed (2001), blended learning focuses on the adoption of the "right" learning techniques for the "right" people at the "right" time and the transfer of the "right" skills to the "right" learning style to optimize academic performance under the learning objectives.

According to Driscoll (2002), blended learning contains four different concepts: 1) The combination of web-based technology modes to achieve an educational goal; 2) The combination of various pedagogical approaches to achieve optimal learning outcomes with or without instructional technology; 3) the combination of any form of instructional technology with face-to-face learning; and 4) the combination of instructional technology with actual job tasks to create a positive learning or work effect.

Whitelock and Jelfs (2003) gave three similar definitions on blended learning: it is the combination of web-based online approaches with traditional face-to-face learning; the combination of media and technology tools applied in an e-learning environment; and the combination of a number of pedagogical approaches, excepting the use of learning technology. Moreover, Neumeier (2005) defined blended learning as "a combination of face-to-face and computer-assisted learning in a single teaching and learning environment" (p. 164). In addition, Bonk and Graham (2012) defined blended learning as the combination of traditional face-to-face instruction with computer-mediated instruction.

Hoic-Bozic (2016) regarded blended learning as the combination of face-to-face classroom learning with internet learning and technology-supported learning to create a more effective learning environment. According to this definition, there are many elements in the learning system that could be blended which include media, technology, online and traditional face-to-face learning environment as well as the blending of different pedagogy.

One of the most cited definition proposed by Garrison and Kanuka (2004) listed as follow:

Blended learning is both simple and complex. At its simplest, blended learning is the thoughtful integration of face-to-face classroom learning experiences with online learning experiences. There is considerable intuitive appeal to the concepts of integrating the strengths of synchronous (face-to-face) and asynchronous (text-based internet) learning activities. At the same time, there is considerable complexity in its implementation with the challenge of virtually limitless design possibilities and applicability to so many contexts. (*p.* 96)

Yoon and Lee (2010) narrowed down the definition of blended learning as "bringing together the positive attributes of online and off-line education, including instructional modalities, delivery methods, learning tools, etc. , concerning language teaching and learning approaches and methods to reinforce the learning process, to bring about the optimal learner achievement, and to enhance the quality of teaching and learning" (p. 180).

Considering the blended core and the complexity in the implementation of blended learning and teaching, designers should consider and decide when and how students need to engage with what kind of digital technology, when and how face-to-face activities should be infused into the face-to-face classroom (Bown, 2019). Blended learning is a learning method that has been developed after traditional face-to-face classroom learning and online learning.

According to Bonk and Graham (2012), the reasons people choose blended learning is first because blended learning provides more effective pedagogical practices. Learners and trainees could firstly use self-paced online learning to acquire background information, then have face-to-face learning focused on applying active learning experiences, finally transfer their knowledge through online learning and support. Particularly, Means et al. (2013) claimed that blended learning has the maximum effect on learners' learning outcomes. Secondly, Blended learning could increase learning access and flexibility. This is one reason people choosing blended learning. Blended learning makes it possible for students to study at a distance in time and space, which makes learners more flexible and convenient to seek additional education. The third reason people choosing blended learning is that it increases cost-effectiveness. It is one of the major goals for blended systems in both higher education and corporation. Corporations could use blended learning to achieve a high return on investment.

The purpose of using the blended learning approach is to "find a harmonious balance between online access to knowledge and face-to-face human interaction" (Osguthorpe & Graham, 2003. p. 228). According to Osguthorpe and Graham (2003), there are six reasons for choosing blended learning: pedagogical richness, access to knowledge, social interaction, personal agency, cost-effectiveness, and ease of revision. As a combination of online and traditional face-to-face learning, blended learning remedies the defects of a single form of instruction and provides more choices for teachers and students (Wang et al., 2019). With the application of information and technology, blended learning has also become a prominent method in higher education (Kim, 2021).

2) *Blended Learning Model in the EFL Context*

Since the most important goal of designing blended learning is to find the most effective combination of two learning modes for different learning subjects, contexts and objectives (Neumeier, 2005), before implementing a blended course, the designers should consider and decide when and how students need to engage with what kind of digital technologies (such as computer-based learning system, mobile applications, web-based project, etc.), when and how face-to-face activities should be infused to the face-to-face classroom (Bown, 2019).

Table 2-8 Parameters Describing and Conceptualizing a Blended Learning Environment for Language Learning and Teaching Purposes

Parameter	Individual descriptors
Mode	Focus on mode
	Distribution of modes
	Choice of mode
Model of integration	Sequencing of individual modes
	Level of integration

续表

Parameter	Individual descriptors
Distribution of learning content and objectives and assignment of purpose	Parallel or isolated
Language teaching methods	Use of teaching methods in each of the modes employed
Involvement of learning subjects (students, tutors and teachers)	Interactional patterns: individual vs. collaborative language learning activity
	Variety of teacher and learner roles
	Level of autonomy
Location	Classroom, home, outdoors, computer room, institutional settings

Source: Neumeier (2005)

When designing a blended learning environment, the most important matter that needs to be considered is which combination of modes could provide the most appropriate form for language teaching and learning. In order to solve the problem, Neumeier (2005) provided parameters for blended learning course designers. The parameters for designing a blended learning course were concluded based on the researcher's empirical experience and theories in Second Language Acquisition (SLA) and Computer-Assisted Language Learning (CALL). They are mode, model of integration, distribution of learning content and objectives and assignment of purpose, language teaching methods, involvement of learning subjects, and location (See Table 2-8).

In Neumeier's (2005) framework, the six parameters are the key factors in designing a foreign language blended learning model. In specific, there are two kinds of learning modes in blended learning, which are face-to-face and computer-assisted. When designing blended learning, the lead mode needs to be first determined. The lead mode is determined according to the time that students spend and the mode that the course is led. The second parameter is the model of integration, which contains sequencing of modes and level of integration. Sequencing of modes means the sequence of the face-to-face mode and the online mode, whether it is alternative, parallel, or overlapping. Level of integration means whether the two modes are compulsory or optional. The third parameter refers to the distribution of learning content and objectives and assignment of purpose is parallel or isolated. Parallel means the learning content and objectives can be implemented either in the face-to-face classroom or the CALL environment. While isolated means the learning content or objective can only be implemented under a single mode. The fourth is the teaching methods employed in each mode. The fifth contains the pattern of interaction between teachers and students, individuals and computers, and the role of teachers and students. The sixth parameter is the location of learning.

Only with careful design and analysis on participants' needs and abilities can blended learning courses foster success in language learning (Neumeier, 2005). Later, the designing framework was applied in a technology-enhanced blended model in an ESL listening and speaking class (Grgurovic, 2011). It was confirmed that the model integrated modes and learning contents successfully.

Sun and Qiu (2017) also developed a framework of blended learning model which integrated the use of online language LMS with traditional face-to-face teaching according to the teaching procedures from Huang et al. (2008) and based on the parameters proposed by

Neumeier (2005). In Figure 2-1, the model consists of three stages, which combines learner' autonomous learning on an LMS and the internet, online collaborative learning with the BBS of the LMS, face-to-face foreign language teaching.

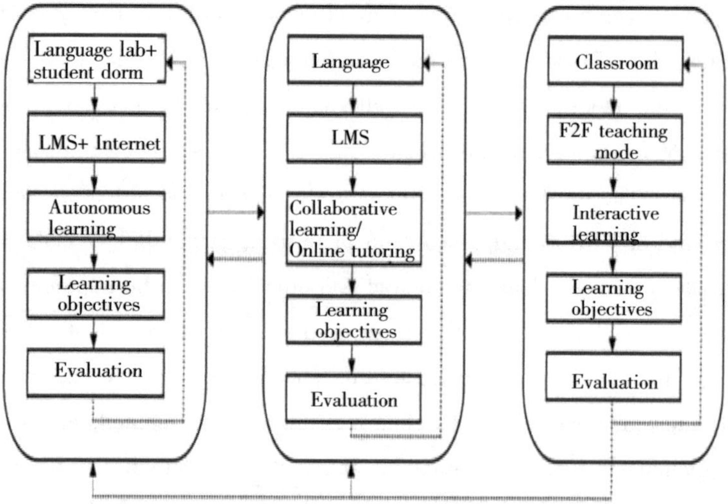

Figure 2-1 A Blended Learning Model for College EFL Class (Sun & Qiu, 2017)

The study investigated the effect of the blended learning model on Chinese EFL students' academic achievement and language proficiency and students' attitude towards a learning approach. Findings showed that the experimental group made significant improvements in their language proficiency level by using the blended learning model. To some extent, it indicated that the blended learning model is suitable to the Chinese EFL class environment. But the validity and reliability were not demonstrated in the study although a questionnaire was used to investigate students' attitudes towards the blended learning model. Moreover, the blended model did not show a direct connection with

Neumeier's (2005) six parameters for designing a blended learning EFL course. It did not provide an appropriate model for language teachers to follow.

Yu and Du (2019) adopted a blended learning model into a content-based EFL curriculum. By exploring the effect of the blended learning model in such a curriculum, it expanded and enriched the empirical research in content-based instruction (CBI). It firstly described the learning environment that the blended learning model existed. Then it decided the resources provided in the online learning library (such as micro-lectures, news, interviews, lectures from TED, movies, relevant books, etc.). The blended learning model integrated online learning with face-to-face learning together (Shown in Figure 2-2).

To be specific, the online learning session was viewed as the input session, which was designed based on four types of learning approaches (autonomous learning, task-based learning, collaborative learning, and interactive learning). Meanwhile, the face-to-face learning session was viewed as the output session, which was designed based on the CBI six T's framework (theme, text, topic, tread, task, and transition). After the experiment, a comparative analysis was conducted between the experimental group and the control group. The results showed that EFL students from the experimental group achieved effective and significant improvement in their academic performance.

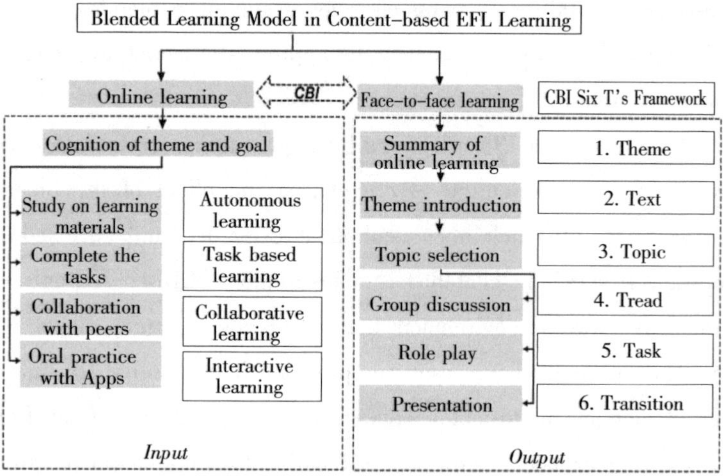

Figure 2-2　Blended Learning Model in Content-based EFL Learning (Yu & Du, 2019)

Moreover, students were reported to have an increase in learning engagement and improvement. In the study, students' improvement was compared under the blended learning model and the conventional face-to-face learning model. It had been proved that EFL students could gain more improvements in their learning engagement, academic performance in listening and speaking. This study provided a blended language model based on a certain language approach, and it contributed detailed suggestions on the strategies and materials which could be used in a blended learning environment. However, the blended learning model was based on CBI teaching methods. Whether it could have the same effects by using other language teaching methods still need to be further explored.

Cui (2014) designed a blended learning model for Chinese college EFL listening and speaking course which emphasized the hybrid of cooperative learning and autonomous learning. The blended model integrated traditional face-to-face teaching with cooperative online learning under a language learning management system (LMS), which was shown in Figure 2-3.

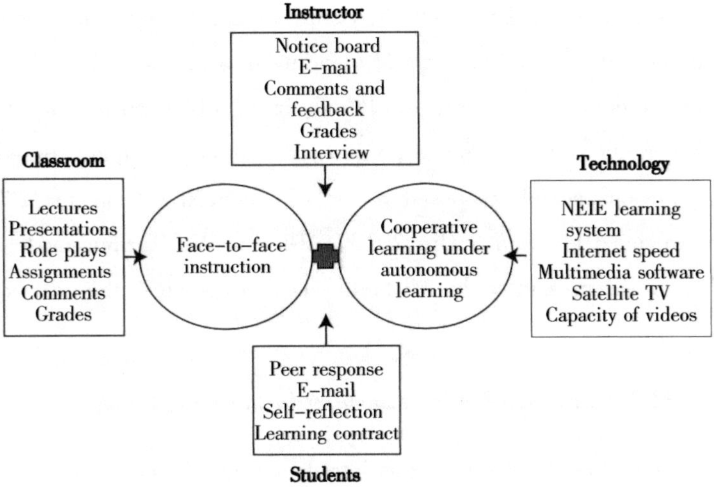

Figure 2-3 Blended Learning Model by Cui (2014)

Under this model, the basic procedure for each unit was divided into three parts: before class, during class, and after class. Time, place, tasks and relevant auxiliaries for each phase and mode were described in the procedure. Cooperative and autonomous are the main forms of online learning. It also presented the contents in traditional face-to-face teaching and cooperative learning under autonomous learning. Teaching tasks for instructors and learning tasks for students were also shown in the blended model. The model integrated online learning and traditional face-to-face learning well. But the tasks for the instructor and students were not classified in detail according to different modes of learning.

From the previous literature related to the blended model, it has revealed that teachers have been viewed "as guides in online learning and monitors in the classroom" under a blended learning environment (Cheung et al. ,2019. p. 44). Even though there have been various studies on blended EFL courses, it still needs to redesign the blended structure and decide the ways of blending in a new situation with different students. The present study redesigned a blended learning model according to the needs and proficiency level of participants based on the previous models proposed in the EFL context (Neumeier, 2005; Grgurovic, 2011; Sun & Qiu, 2017). The blended learning model applied in the present study will be discussed in detail in the next chapter.

3) *Studies on Blended Learning in the EFL Context*

Since blended learning was introduced into the educational field, there have been many studies that attempt to apply it in English language teaching (Grurovic, 2011; Neumeier, 2005; Shih, 2010; Yoon & Lee, 2010). In order to improve students' learning outcomes, many EFL teachers have adopted blended learning in their teaching and investigated its effectiveness (Albiladi & Alshareef, 2019).

Grgurovic (2011) investigated how face-to-face learning integrated with distance learning in an ESL listening and speaking course. One English teacher and 19 ESL students participated in the study. By language class observation, students' questionnaires and teacher interviews, the effectiveness of the blended learning model was explored. The result showed that blended learning could be successfully used to teach all language skills. Both students and teachers held positive attitudes and opinions towards the use of blended learning in teaching English , and they believed that the integration of online learning with traditional face-to-face teaching could improve students' language learning process.

Adas and Bakir (2013) studied the development of EFL students' writing ability by applying blended learning strategies. The study examined whether blended learning could help students to improve their writing skills. 60 EFL students participated in the study and they were divided into two groups: one group adapted traditional face-to-face teaching, and another group adapted blended learning mode. At the end of the course, results showed that the blended learning group performed better on writing than the face-to-face mode group. Meanwhile, improvements in all aspects of writing such as spelling, punctuation, grammar, and paragraph cohesion through blended learning were also confirmed.

Ghazizadeh and Fatemipour (2017) studied the effect of blended learning on the development of EFL learners' reading ability. It explored whether blended learning could improve Iranian EFL students' reading ability by comparing the experimental group with the control group. The experimental group received both classroom instruction and blended learning, while the control group received traditional instruction. Both groups were given pre-test and post-test to measure students' reading ability. The result showed that learners who used blended learning significantly improved their reading proficiency. It confirmed that there was a direct impact on learners' reading ability by using the blended learning model.

During the implementation of blended learning, the effect of students' psychology and behavior could also be influenced by the blended learning environment (Banditvilai, 2016; Munan et al., 2012; Yoon & Lee, 2010). Banditvilai (2016) adopted blended learning to enhance university students' autonomy and language skills. It was pointed out that traditional classroom teaching can no longer meet the needs of individual learning under the modern technology environment. Therefore, an e-learning lesson was developed which was in parallel with the conventional face-to-face language classroom. It was found that online practice in the e-learning lesson was directly beneficial to enhance students' four language skills. It was also found that learning motivation and learning autonomy were effectively enhanced by using a blended learning model.

Yoon and Lee (2010) investigated students' perceptions and effects of blended learning as a teaching strategy in an ESL writing class. Students from 47 universities took part in a 16-week blended learning course on writing. According to the results of pre-test and post-test, it was indicated that students held a positive attitude and perceptions towards the use of blended learning in the L2 writing course and they believed that it is a helpful learning method that can promote their learning motivation and interaction. With the increase of students' learning motivation, their interaction, autonomy and collaboration were also enhanced by applying the blended approach. Finally, the study pointed out that blended learning allows students to interact both in and outside the classroom environment, which increased students' motivation and engagement in learning.

Agustin (2019) proposed five dimensions of student engagement which contained students' positive body language, consistent focus, verbal participation, students' confidence, and fun and excitement by a blended learning instruction implemented in an EFL context. In this study, blended learning instruction was found to foster more students' engagement. And it was found that there were five characteristics of students' engagement that appeared in a face-to-face classroom while the characteristics of engagement in online learning were demonstrated in only two.

One of the significant benefits of blended learning in the EFL context lies in the improvement of students' language learning environment (Albiladi & Alshareef, 2019). Neumeier (2005) proposed a framework for designing a blended learning environment. Six parameters were regarded to be necessary components in a blended learning environment, which were mode, model of integration, distribution of learning content and objectives and assignment of purpose, language teaching methods, involvement of learning subjects, and location.

Ja'ashan (2015) investigated the perceptions and attitudes of EFL students towards a blended course at Bisha University. In order to understand students' perceptions and attitudes, 130 undergraduate students participated in the survey. The results showed that students held positive views on the application of blended learning and were satisfied with the teaching method. Because they believed that blended learning can improve their language proficiency, enhance teacher-student interaction, improve the learning process, and have an interesting learning experience. However, the researchers also pointed out that the disadvantages of blended learning were that it required teachers to spend more time preparing and implementing the blended course, and teaching activities needed to be carried out in two modes.

The researchers concluded that participants reported blended learning was more convenient than conventional face-to-face instruction and increased their learning motivation.

(1) Studies on Blended Learning in Chinese EFL Context

Under the Chinese EFL context, Liu (2013) studied the effectiveness of blended learning in an academic English writing course at a major university in Beijing. It evaluated the course design, material presentation, student participation and classroom evaluation in blended learning. From students' evaluation and teachers' reflection, students highly approved of the use of the blended learning strategy because it had many advantages in promoting autonomy learning, increasing classroom interaction, eliminating communication anxiety, and improving students' academic writing proficiency. It was concluded that as allowing for two different types of learning interactions, blended learning was more motivating for language learners.

In addition, Cui (2014) investigated the effectiveness of a blended learning approach aimed at improving students' listening and speaking skills. A blended learning model was developed based on Neumeier's (2005) six parameters at each phase of listening and speaking teaching. Students' listening proficiency was measured by the listening test in CET-4 and the results showed that students in a blended learning environment achieved better improvement than those in a conventional classroom environment. Moreover, students' speaking ability was improved in both traditional and blended environments, but students in the experimental group showed more significant improvement. In addition, students' initiative and autonomy could also be enhanced in a blended learning environment.

Liu (2016) conducted a blended course that included online autonomous learning, flipped learning, and face-to-face learning to enhance students' learning autonomy and language proficiency. The case study showed that students achieved more effective improvement in their autonomy than that under the situation of face-to-face learning, in turns students' listening and speaking proficiency were improved.

Mu et al. (2019) conducted an empirical study that divided the teaching activities into autonomy learning activities, interactive learning activities and expanding learning activities. In the study, the importance of teacher support on students' learning participation was emphasized. The results showed that the frequency of students' access to lecture materials closely related to the tests was obviously higher than other materials and the interactive learning activities in the classroom could significantly improve students' positive participation in the learning activity.

Huang (2016) explored Chinese EFL students' perceptions of blended learning. Students' attitudes towards a blended English course were analyzed and the results showed that students held a positive attitude on blended learning. They thought online learning and face-to-face learning played different roles in language learning. Online learning was more effective for listening and face-to-face learning could enhance learners' cognition and enhance their interests in learning English. It emphasized the importance to consider how both modes integrate under a blended learning context.

Zhang and Zhu (2018) compared the blended learning model

with the traditional face-to-face model. The sample included 5,376 ESL students from a major university in Beijing. Taking into account the learners' grades, gender, age and subject, the results showed that students who learn in a blended learning environment have higher academic performance than those who learn in a traditional learning environment. It was believed that blended learning has a positive effect on students' learning outcomes.

All the literature reviewed above gives positive perspective views of the effect of blended learning in a foreign language context. In reviewing the literature related to blended learning, one of the significant benefits of blended learning in the EFL context lies in the improvement of students' language learning environment (Albiladi & Alshareef, 2019). The effectiveness of blended learning suggests that a systematic and comprehensive blended learning environment could promote student engagement and positive psychological influence, which could also promise effective achievement in EFL students' language proficiency. Therefore, blended learning is not only one-way learning by students or simple teaching implemented by teachers. What's more, an effective blended learning environment depends more on the design and implementation of teacher's instruction. It could be concluded that it is necessary for the current study to take blended learning as a learning context to explore the effects of teacher support on different variables under such a new environment.

4) *Blended Learning Model in Current Study*

By analyzing different blended models under the Chinese EFL context, the researcher in the current study adopted the blended model in Cui's (2014) study as the most appropriate model because both courses included the objectives of developing students' listening proficiency. The blended model in the current study was shown in Figure 2-4.

Because the current study planned to explore the effects of different types of teacher support on EFL students' learning engagement, learning attitude, and English listening proficiency within a blended learning environment. That means it was needed to create the same basic blended learning environment for the current study. Moreover, Cui (2014) provided not only the blended model of the course but also the blended learning procedures based on Neumeier's (2005) framework of designing a blended language learning environment.

Based on Cui's (2014) model, the researcher in the current study developed the original model by changing the cooperative learning under autonomous learning into online learning based on the LMS. In addition, considering the role of teacher and students, the teaching task for the teacher and the learning task for students were divided into the online learning tasks and the face-to-face tasks. What's more, the researcher added a circle between traditional face-to-face learning and online learning because it indicated that the learning contents and instructional activities were connected and organized in a parallel structure.

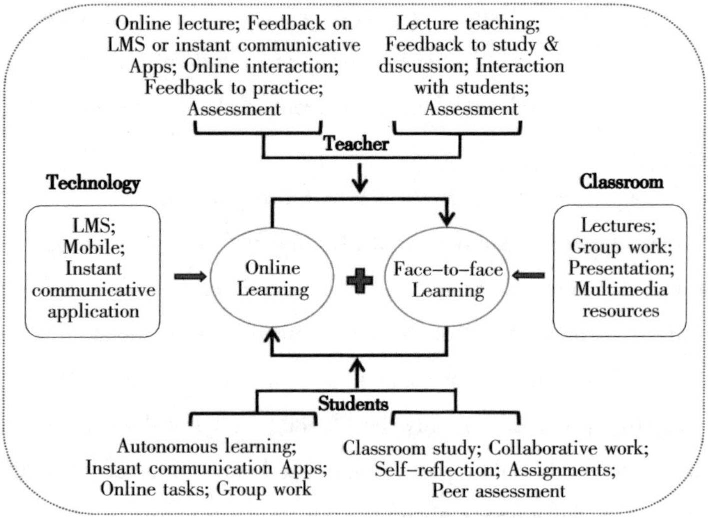

Figure 2-4 Blended Learning Model for EFL Learning

(Modified based on Cui (2014))

Together with the revised blended learning model, a relevant blended learning procedure was provided in Table 2-9. According to the online learning mode and face-to-face learning mode, each unit of the course was divided into three phases, which are Before Class, During Class, and After Class. Time distribution in two modes, place for learning, tasks and auxiliaries under each mode was described in the procedure. It illustrated the different procedures to be followed for each phase.

Table 2-9 Blended Learning Procedure of the Present EFL Course

	Before Class	During Class		After Class
Time	Two period (100 mins)	Two period (100 mins)	Two period (100 mins)	Flexible

续表

	Before Class	During Class		After Class
Place	Flexible	Classroom	Classroom	Flexible
Tasks	Autonomous learning, Search and collect topic related information, Cooperative activities, Online exercises, Online test, Discussion	Face-to-face lecture, Individual task	Paired work, Group work, Role play, Presentation Assessment	Skill practice, Group work, Learning Feedback, Assessment
Auxiliaries	LMS, QQ, Wechat, Websites, Mobile phone	Computer, Projector, Video, Audio, Textbook	Computer, Projector, Video, Audio, Mobile phone	LMS, QQ, Wechat, Mobile phone

In the Before Class phase, students need to study the online lecture on the LMS where they might also receive requirements and assignments from the teacher. In this part, students had autonomous online lecture learning tasks and group tasks with their classmates. During Class, the first two periods are face-to-face lectures in a multimedia language lab, followed by another two periods of face-to-face paired work, group work, role plan, and presentation in the multimedia language lab. In the After Class phase, students had homework and new assignment related to the unit content via the LMS platform. Teachers also gave feedback and discussed with students by other instant information applications, like QQ, and WeChat. Students in the present study spent 34% of their time in the online mode and 66% of their time in the face-to-face mode. The learning contents were organized in a parallel way and the online resources were closely connected with the skills practiced in the classroom and closely followed the organization of the textbook.

6. Summary

In this chapter, as the independent variable in the study, teacher support was analyzed from three different types: namely, teacher's autonomy support, emotional support, and cognitive support. Each type of teacher support has been regarded as an important factor in improving students' engagement, language proficiency, or learning attitude. Therefore, the effectiveness of teacher support was reviewed.

Then students' learning engagement was reviewed. In this part, Fredricks et al.'s (2004) three dimensions of learning engagement were adopted in the present study, which are behavioral engagement, emotional engagement, and cognitive engagement. In addition, factors influencing learning engagement were analyzed. Among those factors, teacher support is one of the most important factors which could influence learning engagement. Meanwhile, studies related to learning engagement were reviewed because they provided more perspectives in promoting students' achievements.

In addition, learners' learning attitude was been discussed in this part. Two factors—students' self-confidence and language anxiety—were proved to be closely related to students' affective factors. Under the influence of teacher support, these two factors in learners' learning attitudes will directly influence students' language achievements.

As one of the dependent variables, English listening proficiency was put into the reviewing list. By reviewing the previous literature, it explained why it was important to improve EFL students' listening proficiency. Regarding Chinese university EFL students being weak in their listening proficiency and their difficulties in English listening, the researcher analyzed previous studies related to EFL listening proficiency and found that teacher's instruction and supportive behavior were some of the key factors influencing students' listening proficiency. Therefore, it is necessary to investigate the effects of teacher support on students' English listening proficiency in the current study.

Blended learning, as the product of technology development, has been widely applied in higher education. It is also the learning environment under which the current study had been conducted. Therefore, the author chose the most appropriate definition based on the previous literature which is also widely accepted. Reasons for choosing blended learning were explained. Moreover, studies on blended learning in the EFL context were reviewed. It has been confirmed that blended learning could develop students' language proficiency, increase students' motivation and engagement, and improve the learning environment. Since the current study adopted a blended learning environment, it is necessary to study from other successful models in the EFL context. The current study will analyze and present its blended learning model based on the previous studies on the blended learning and teaching model.

Overall, based on the previous literature, the current study attempts to explore the effects of different types of teacher support on students' learning engagement, listening proficiency, and learning attitude when these teacher supports come to students separately, and which types of teacher support will be more effective.

第三章　研究方法

本章介绍了实施该研究的整体步骤及实施过程和对研究参与者(即学生)的描述及分组情况,并着重介绍在研究过程中教师实施的三种不同类型的教师支持行为如何分别作用于不同小组。基于实施分组教学对比,研究者所采用的问卷及测试的信效度、数据分析方法和过程也会在本章进行逐一介绍。

Chapter 3 Methodology

The purpose of this study was to investigate the effects of different types of teacher support—emotional support, cognitive support, autonomy support—on Chinese EFL students' learning engagement, language learning attitude, and listening proficiency in a blended learning environment. This chapter is mainly concerned with the methodology adopted in this research. It describes the research procedure, participants, variables of the study, instruments, and a description of how data were analyzed to address the research questions mentioned in Chapter I.

1. Overall Research Procedure

The present study adopted a pretest-treatment-posttest structure with three experimental groups to explore the effect of different types of teacher support on Chinese university EFL students' engagement, language learning attitude and listening proficiency under a blended learning environment. The independent variable, three different types of teacher support, represents the treatment of the experiment.

Firstly, to investigate the effect of different types of teacher support under the same basic context, a blended learning model for course learning was developed based on students' needs and curriculum objectives(See Chapter II). Under the same blended learning environment, three types of teacher supportive behaviors were each implemented into the blended learning model.

Secondly, the course in the present study employed three intact classes. The classes were assigned as three experimental groups at random which were the emotional support group (ES, n = 22), the cognitive support group (CS, n = 22), and the autonomy support group (AS, n = 22).

Thirdly, at the first week of the blended course, structured questionnaire-based surveys were conducted as pre-surveys to examine participants' learning engagement and language learning attitude. In addition, a pre-test on participants' listening proficiency was also conducted to explore the level of students' listening proficiency before the treatment.

Fourthly, different types of teacher support were given to different experimental groups from the second week to the sixteenth week of the blended course. All groups studied the course under the same blended learning environment. The only difference was the type of support given to each group. As such, the differences in students' engagement level, language learning attitude level as reflected in the post-survey and listening proficiency in the post-test can be attributed to the treatment itself.

Fifthly, at the seventeenth week of the course, post-surveys on EFL students' learning engagement and language learning attitude were conducted again. In addition, a post-test on EFL students' listening proficiency was implemented as well.

Table 3-1 Research Procedure of Current Study

Process	Week	Experimental Group		
		ES	CS	AS
Before the experiment	1	Pre-survey (Learning Engagement)		
		Pre-survey (Attitude Questionnaire)		
		Pre-test (CET Listening Test)		
During the experiment	2-16	Emotional support	Cognitive support	Autonomy support
After the experiment	17	Post-survey (Learning Engagement)		
		Post-survey (Attitude Questionnaire)		
		Post-test (CET Listening Test)		

At last, data collected in the pre-survey and post-survey was analyzed to determine whether students' behavioral engagement, cognitive engagement, and emotional engagement were enhanced under the influence of different types of teacher support. Other pre-survey and post-survey data on EFL students' language learning attitude was also analyzed to explore whether there were differences in EFL students' language learning attitude as a result of different types of teacher support. Then, the pre-test and post-test data on students' listening proficiency was analyzed to examine the effects of different types of teacher support on their listening proficiency. The experimental process was shown in Table 3-1.

2. Participants

In order to improve EFL students' learning engagement, learning attitude, and listening proficiency, 66 junior students in English major took part in this empirical study. The reason for choosing students in English major was because as part of Chinese EFL learners, students in English major have more chance to apply English in school, but their listening proficiency is still lower than other language proficiency (Zou et al., 2012). All participants were from T University, a public university in Southwest China, and aged from 20 to 25. They had experienced English education as a foreign language for at least 9 consecutive years from primary school to high school. In Table 3-2, participants in the current study were distributed in three intact classes. To compare the extent to which participants were influenced by different types of teacher support, participants in the three classes were randomly assigned as the emotional support (ES, n = 22), cognitive support (CS, n = 22), and autonomy support (AS, n = 22).

Table 3-2 Participants

Group	Age		Gender		English Learning Experience	Blended Learning Experience
	20-22	23-25	Male	Female		
ES (n = 22)	18	4	2	20	Over 9 consecutive years	At least one blended course
CS (n = 22)	17	5	2	20		
AS (n = 22)	18	4	2	20		

All participants were enrolled in an English interpreting course that met once a week for 100 minutes over 17 weeks from February 22nd of 2021 to June 18th of 2021 at T University. The course was compulsory for junior students majoring in English at the university. Students were required to study and master the skills of listening comprehension, interpreting memorization, note-taking, public speaking, etc.. More specifically, by the end of the course, students are expected to identify the key words in speeches, grasp the main idea and retell most of the information of the original speeches, then accurately translate the meaning that the speaker wants to convey. In particular, the course is designed to help students master the skills of identifying key words, listening to the main idea, note-taking, retelling, analyzing discourse, public speaking, and translating. All participants in the current study were taught by the same researcher. They were not told that they were taking part in an experiment. It was deliberately designed to reduce the subtle effects of participants knowing that they are in an experimental group and which experimental group they were in, which might damage the validity of the experiment (Cohen et al., 2007).

3. Variables of the Study

Considering the expected objectives, enhancing EFL students' learning engagement, learning attitude and listening proficiency are the priority to be taken into consideration. Since the first step in interpreting is listening and understanding the speaker's speech, this course was built based on listening in exploring the effects of teacher support on improving students' learning engagement, learning attitude and listening proficiency.

Table 3-3 Variables of the Study

Independent Variable	Dependent Variable
Teacher support	Students' learning engagement · Behavioral engagement · Cognitive engagement · Emotional engagement
	Students' attitudes toward language learning · Self-confidence · Language anxiety
	Student' English listening proficiency

In Table 3-3, the independent variable is teacher support represented in three different types: emotional support, cognitive support and autonomy support. The experimental groups were each treated with different types of teacher supportive behaviors by the researcher to promote their learning engagement, listening proficiency, and attitude.

As for the dependent variables, the first dependent variable is represented in students' learning engagement, including behavioral engagement, cognitive engagement and emotional engagement. Students' learning engagement was determined by the extent and types of teacher support given to them during blended learning and was measured before and after the treatment. The second dependent variable is EFL students' language learning attitudes towards teacher support before and after the experiment, which includes the investigation on students' self-confidence and language anxiety. The third dependent variable is students' listening proficiency which is measured by the pre-test and post-test in the listening part of CET-4 examinations. All participants attended the course and participated in the pre-survey and post-surveys and tests.

4. Operational Behaviors of Teacher Support in the Blended Course

1) Different Teacher Support Operational Behaviors

Teacher support in the current study contains teacher emotional support, cognitive support, and autonomy support. Three experimental groups represent three types of teacher support. In Chapter II, different teacher support operational behaviors had been extracted from previous literature. In addition, based on the same blended course model and blended learning procedures of the current study (see Figure 2-4 and Table 2-9), the current study adopted the following operational behaviors of teacher support in the three phases of the blended course to each experimental group.

(1) Teacher's Supportive Behaviors Before Class

In the Before Class phase, students need to search and collect topic-related information from the online resources and have autonomous learning on the online lecture through the LMS. In addition, they will discuss the learning topic with their classmates and the teacher through the LMS or other instant communication applications. Moreover, relevant tests are provided to examine their learning. and According to students' learning tasks at this phase, the teacher implemented different types of teacher support operational behaviors based on the basic learning contents, which are shown in Table 3-4.

Table 3-4 Three Types of Teacher's Supportive Behaviors Before Class

	Before Class (Online Learning)
Emotional Support Operational Behaviors	Providing encouragement to students' online study Expressing expectation on students' study Giving praise on students' online performance Participating discussion with students Giving comments and feedback to students' views
Cognitive Support Operational Behaviors	Providing learning strategy Stimulating students' curiosity Providing students with challenging but achievable tasks Connecting learning contents with students' real-life experiences Using multimedia resources to create a language learning environment
Autonomy Support Operational Behaviors	Providing diversified resources Low controlling behavior Providing appropriate opportunities for students' academic activities Giving students enough freedom in choosing learning content Providing opportunities to express themselves

For the emotional support group, the teacher firstly expresses his or her expectation on what students are going to learn and master. The teacher needs to actively participate in online discussions with students and gives prompt feedback or comments to students' opinions. In addition, the teacher needs to praise and encourage students' online performance to enhance their learning confidence.

As for the cognitive support group, the teacher needs to provide learning material which is connecting the learning contents with students' real-life experience and try to stimulate students' learning curiosity. Moreover, the teacher needs to use multimedia resources to create a language learning environment for students to have online discussions with each other and with the teacher. Regarding the online learning lecture, the teacher could provide some language learning strategies to help students master the language points. At the end of the online learning section, the teacher should provide students with challenging but achievable tasks.

Regarding the autonomy support group, the teacher needs to provide more diversified learning resources according to students' language proficiency. Meanwhile, students are allowed to arrange and choose the learning contents. The teacher should also try to provide appropriate opportunities for students' language learning activities even in the online learning section. In online discussions, the teacher should allow students to express themselves. In addition, controlling behavior should avoid during the teaching process.

(2) Teacher's Supportive Behaviors During Class

In the During Class phase, students are going to have face-to-face lecture learning, and need to finish individual tasks based on the lecture. Moreover, students are going to have cooperative work with their classmates, such as paired work, group work, and role play. In class, students will have the chance to make presentations on their own work and group work. Table 3-5 presents the operational supportive behaviors in different types of teacher support groups.

Considering students' learning tasks in the face-to-face section, the teacher needs to provide different operational supportive behavior to different experimental groups. When comes to the emotional support group, the teacher could try to create a positive learning climate to stimulate students learning motivation and enthusiasm. They need to pay positive attention to learners' learning status by inquiring about students' learning situations. The teacher should actively participate in students' discussions and give positive comments on students' views or class performance.

Table 3-5 Three Types of Supportive Teacher Behaviors During Class Time

	During Class (Face-to-face Learning)
Emotional Support Operational Behaviors	· Creating positive learning climate · Stimulating students' learning motivation and enthusiasm · Inquiring for students' learning situation · Participating interaction and discussion with students · Giving praise on students' performance and improvement · Giving positive comments to students' views and performance · Sharing teacher's point of view with students
Cognitive Support Operational Behaviors	· Providing learning strategies related to course subject · Providing students with challenging but achievable tasks · Stimulating students' curiosity by giving examples or raising questions · Connecting learning contents with students' real-life experience · Guiding students to think instead of giving answer directly
Autonomy Support Operational Behaviors	· Designing different learning activities and providing appropriate opportunities for students to participate · Providing students opportunities to express themselves · Accepting students' opinions and feeling · Adjusting the teaching progress according to students' online learning

As for the cognitive support group, when students are studying in class, the teacher needs to provide students with language learning strategies and apply simple ways to explain the skills or concepts in language learning. When giving students assignments or tasks related to the face-to-face lecture, the teacher needs to consider students' proficiency level and provide challenging but achievable tasks. During the process of completing tasks or answering questions, the teacher needs to guide students to think instead of giving answers directly. In addition, the teacher should provide timely help when students have questions about the learning contents.

Regarding the autonomy support group, the teacher needs to design different learning activities and provide more opportunities for students to participate. Meanwhile, the teacher needs to provide opportunities for every student to express themselves and try to accept students' opinions and feelings. Considering the situation of students' online learning, the teacher should adjust the teaching progress correspondingly.

(3) Teacher's Supportive Behaviors After Class

In the After Class phase, students turn back to online learning. They are going to have skill and language practice in the LMS. Sometimes they need to make a reflection on their study and make feedback to the teacher. In addition, they are going to work with their group members through the LMS and other instant communication applications. A unit test will be also conducted on students through the online LMS.

In Table 3-6, according to students' learning task in the online learning phase after the face-to-face learning, in the emotional support group, when students have negative learning emotions or fail in the exam, the teacher needs to show their concern and provide encouragement. Although there is no extra course hour at this phase, the teacher needs to provide extra time to help students with their questions. The teacher needs to provide prompt responses and feedback to students' online messages and praise students' improvement and performance.

As for the cognitive support group, the teacher provides students with challenging but achievable tasks according to students' proficiency level. When they have problems in learning, the teacher should provide help. In addition, it will be better to guide students to think rather than give them answers directly. After units study, the teacher should recognize students' efforts in learning.

Table 3-6 Three Types of Teacher's Supportive Behaviors After Class

After Class (Online Learning)	
Emotional Support Operational Behaviors	Supporting students' emotions when they are facing pressure or challenges Spending time in helping students on their questions Giving prompt response and feedback Giving praise on students' improvement and performance
Cognitive Support Operational Behaviors	Providing students with challenging but achievable tasks Recognizing students' efforts in learning Guiding students to think instead of giving answer directly Providing help when students encountering difficulties in learning

续表

After Class (Online Learning)	
Operational Behaviors that Support Autonomy	Providing diversified learning resources Giving students enough freedom in choosing academic tasks Encouraging students to be responsible for their own learning Adjusting teaching progress according to students' autonomous learning

When it comes to autonomy support group, the teacher needs to provide diversified learning resources for students to have more freedom in choosing tasks and learning contents based on their own language proficiency level. When giving students more freedom in tasks choosing, the teacher needs to make students understand they have the responsibility for their own learning. Moreover, considering students' face-to-face learning situation and students' performance in classroom learning and online learning, the teacher needs to adjust the teaching contents and progress correspondently. At the three different learning phases in the blended course, the teacher needs to conduct different types of teacher supportive behaviors according to the above framework.

2) *Expert Validation*

To examine the feasibility of the framework of different teacher supportive behaviors under the blended course, five experts were invited to review the blended course model and different frameworks for teacher supportive behaviors. Four experts were invited and they communicated with the researcher on the study by interviews. Together with their review the basic blended model and different frameworks on teacher supportive behaviors, experts gave comments and suggestions on different frameworks of teacher supportive behaviors and on the current study. Another Korean expert (K) reviewed the study and framework and gave comments by email.

The expert review mainly focused on the operational behaviors of different types of teacher support according to the basic blended learning model of the current course. They all suggested that the teacher needs to always focus on the supportive behaviors provided to different experimental groups. Their comments were presented as follows:

"*The three types of teacher support operational behavior framework under the blended learning environment have been well designed by the researcher. It should be implemented strictly following this framework during the course implementation*" (*Expert A*).

"*Under the blended learning environment, teacher's supportive behaviors have the feature of diversity and randomness. Therefore, when implementing the blended course with different types of teacher support, the teacher should be able to adopt different operational behaviors flexibly and diversely according to students' needs*" (*Expert D*).

By accepting from experts' opinions, the current study analyzed students' learning tasks during the three phases of the blended course and then chose proper operational behaviors based on the previous study listed in Chapter II. It can be regarded that the current teacher support operational behavior framework had been confirmed on its validity and feasibility.

5. Instruments

1) Students' Learning Engagement Questionnaire

Since the current study was conducted within a blended learning environment, in order to investigate the changes of EFL students' learning engagement after the treatment of different types of teacher support in the blended learning environment, Blended Learning Student Engagement Scale (BLSES) from Ma et al. (2017) was adopted. Students' learning engagement was investigated and analyzed from behavioral, emotional and cognitive aspects which contain six factors in students' active learning, teacher-student interaction, group work, implementing learning strategies, self-regulation, and emotional involvement.

Ma et al. (2017) constructed an initial item pool framework of student engagement based on the characteristics of blended learning, definition and dimensions of student engagement. A pilot study, validity analysis, and factor analysis of the scale resulted in a total of 29 items, with 13 behavioral engagement items, 10 cognitive engagement items, and 6 emotional engagement items. The items were scored on a five-point Likert scale, in which "never" scoring 1, "seldom" scoring 2, "sometimes" scoring 3, "often" scoring 4, and "always" scoring 5.

Based on the initial item pool, Ma and Zhou (2019) conducted an empirical study on student engagement dimensions and factors in a blended learning environment. Through the difference significance test on each item and the analysis of the Cronbach's Alpha estimate of the scale ($\alpha=0.928$), 27 items remained, in which there were 13 behavioral engagement items, 9 cognitive engagement items, and 5 emotional engagement items. Six factors were extracted from the Exploratory Factor Analysis (EFA) of behavioral engagement, cognitive engagement, and emotional engagement. The six factors were active learning, teacher-student interaction, group work, implementing learning strategy, self-regulation, and emotional involvement. In the Confirmatory Factor Analysis (CFA), this 27-item scale was also proved to be a model with a good fit.

Because of the different educational backgrounds of participants, the present study adopted Ma and Zhou's (2019) 27-item BLSES and made some minor adjustments to the scale. Such as, the original item "I used web-based learning system to communicate with other students" was changed into "I used web-based learning system or other instant message applications to communicate with other students about English learning"; the original item "I use what I learned to solve practical problems in blended learning" was changed into "I use what I learned to solve practical language problems in blended course"; the original item "Blended learning could stimulate my enthusiasm for learning" was changed into "Blended learning could stimulate my enthusiasm for English learning"; and the original item "I feel pleasure when learning this blended course" was changed as "I feel pleasure when learning this blended English course".

To ensure students fully understand the survey questions, the BLSES was translated into Chinese using the following procedures: Firstly, the researcher (who is Chinese-English bilingual) translated the BLSES into Chinese, and then the translated version was cross-checked by another Chinese-English bilingual teacher. After the cross-check, they met and discussed with each other to revise the discrepancies which occurred between them. Then the Chinese version of BLSES was validated by four English major students on their understanding of each item. To check the accuracy of translation and ensure validity, three experts in English-Chinese translation were invited to check the translation of every item in the scale.

Considering the different backgrounds of the participants and the minor adjustments on some items, EFA and CFA analyses were conducted again based on the data in the current study. In the EFA analysis, a total of 314 online questionnaires were distributed and collected through WenJuanxing online survey system. Excluding students who answered "no" to the question of whether they had a blended learning experience and those with suspected unreal answers, 273 valid questionnaires were retained, with 86.94% efficiency. 186 questionnaires were used for the EFA, and 87 questionnaires for CFA.

(1) Exploratory Factor Analysis

The scale was composed of behavioral engagement, cognitive engagement, and emotional engagement. There were 13 items in behav ioral engagement, which mainly related to students' active learning and interaction with teachers and peers in blended learning; there were 9 items in cognitive engagement, which mainly contained the index of self-learning strategies and self-regulation; there were 5 items in emotional engagement, which included the feeling of pleasure, joy and excitement and belongings during blended learning.

Table 3-7 Rotated Component Matrix[a]

	Component					
	1	2	3	4	5	6
Item2	0.038	0.781	0.057	0.269	0.136	0.158
Item3	-0.007	0.763	0.102	-0.026	0.118	0.215
Item5	0.117	0.757	0.162	0.112	0.192	0.153
Item8	0.087	0.745	0.082	0.207	0.031	0.143
Item6	0.125	0.712	0.101	0.270	0.070	0.096
Item12	0.110	0.643	0.214	0.257	0.147	-0.048
Item15	0.203	0.218	0.115	0.714	0.162	0.172
Item22	-0.060	0.157	0.108	0.712	0.111	0.249
Item21	0.130	0.202	0.139	0.711	0.151	0.038
Item20	0.021	0.251	0.232	0.659	0.070	0.120
Item19	0.185	0.113	0.262	0.649	0.221	0.165
Item14	0.106	0.137	0.080	0.647	0.145	0.300
Item27	0.049	0.080	0.220	0.171	0.180	0.749
Item23	0.048	0.109	-0.011	0.122	0.085	0.724
Item26	0.058	0.164	0.135	0.195	0.101	0.724
Item25	0.106	0.125	0.095	0.135	0.041	0.684
Item24	0.094	0.107	0.157	0.130	0.115	0.646
Item13	0.131	0.183	0.785	0.164	0.030	0.075
Item9	0.107	0.174	0.770	0.209	0.154	0.214
Item11	0.063	0.048	0.711	0.107	0.225	0.105
Item10	0.103	0.214	0.596	0.266	0.039	0.266
Item1	0.811	-0.002	0.082	0.148	-0.066	0.148
Item7	0.808	0.155	0.064	0.071	0.106	0.071
Item4	0.661	0.162	0.186	0.105	0.136	0.105
Item18	0.099	0.185	0.137	0.173	0.801	0.173
Item16	0.107	0.128	0.137	0.329	0.677	0.329
Item17	-0.015	0.178	0.175	0.213	0.668	0.213

Extraction Method: Principal Component Analysis.

Rotation Method: Varimax with Kaiser Normalization.

a. Rotation converged in 5 iteration.

In EFA, when KMO >0.08, it indicates that factor analysis is appropriate for the current scale. When the Bartlett's test <0.05, it indicates a significance of the data, which means the current data is proper for factor analysis. In the current study, the KMO is 0.896 and the Bartlett' test is 0.000, both indicated that the data and scale is suitable for factor analysis.

By extracting the common factor whose eigenvalues is over 1 in the Principle Component Analysis (PCA), and adopting orthogonal rotation to make factor analysis on behavioral engagement, cognitive engagement, and emotional engagement respectively, three factors were converged in behavioral engagement, two factors were converged in cognitive engagement, and one factor was under emotional engagement.

According to the study of Ma and Zhou (2019), they named each factor based on previous theoretical background. The current study was extracted and converged the same factors. Therefore, each factor was given the same name as in Ma and Zhou's study. Factor 1 was named "group work" (including E1, E4, E7), which measures students' performance in collaborative group learning with their peers. Factor 2 was named "teacher-student interaction" (including E2, E3, E5, E6, E8, E12), which mainly investigates the interaction between students and teacher, and between students and their peers. Factor 3 was named "active learning" (including E9, E10, E11, E13), which measures students' performance in completing learning activities and tasks. Factor 4 was named "implementing learning strategy" (including E14, E15, E19, E20, E21, E22), which unveils how students apply cognitive strategies in their learning in a blended learning environment. Factor 5 was named "self-regulation" (including E16,E17,E18), which reflects how students plan and manage their learning in a blended learning environment. Factor 6 was named "emotional involvement" (including E23, E24, E25, E26, E27), which focuses on students' attitudes, feeling and group belongings in a blended learning environment.

Under each factor, different items were included. The reliability of the total scale and each factor is shown below Table 3-8. The total reliability of the scale is 0.919, and the Cronbach's value of all factors was over 0.07, which demonstrated an ideal reliability of the current scale.

Table 3-8 Internal Consistency Coefficient and KMO

Dimensions	Factors	Item number	KMO	Cronbach's α	
Behavioral engagement	Group work	3	0.858	0.710	0.860
	Teacher-student interaction	6		0.876	
	Active learning	4		0.800	
Cognitive engagement	Implementing learning strategy	6	0.882	0.855	0.866
	Self-regulation	3		0.746	
Emotional engagement	Emotional involvement	5	0.839	0.806	0.806
Total scale		27			

(2) Confirmatory Factor Analysis

Based on the EFA on the BLSES, the present study adopted Amos 23.0 to conduct a Confirmatory Factor Analysis (CFA) on the collected data to confirm the proposed six-factor (three behavioral engagement, two cognitive engagement, and one emotional engagement variables).

Table 3-9 CFA Model Parameter on Engagement Scale

CMIN	df	CMIN/DF	NFI	IFI	TLI	CFI	GFI	RMSEA
319.938	309	1.035	0.846	0.994	0.993	0.994	0.801	0.020
Suggested value		<3	>0.8	>0.9	>0.8	>0.9	>0.8	<0.08

When evaluating model fit, various fit indices are recommended. When the root mean square error of approximation (RSMEA) is lower than 0.08 and the NFI and comparative fit index (CFI) are higher than 0.09, it indicates a good model fit (Kelloway, 1998; Kline, 2004). The Cronbach's α was 0.927 and the CFA results ($x2/df$ = 1.035, CFI = 0.994, TLI = 0.993, RMSEA = 0.020,) both showed that the scale was with good reliability and validity (See Table 3-9).

The EFA and CFA had proved the reliability and validity of the Blended Learning Student Engagement Scale (BLSES). In the current study, this scale was firstly used as the pre-survey to investigate all participants' levels of learning engagement before the blended course. After a 15-week study on the blended course, this scale was used again as the post-survey to examine all participants' engagement levels at week 17.

2) *Students' Language Learning Attitude Questionnaire*

Language learning attitude is closely related to language learning (Starks &Paltridge, 1996) and learners' learning attitude is one of the most critical factors determining the success of language learning (Ehrman et al. 2003). Regarding learners' self-confidence and language learning anxiety are the two important emotional factors in learning attitude (Zhang & Yuan, 2004), the present study investigated the effects of teacher support on EFL students' language learning attitude from the aspect of students' self-confidence and language anxiety respectively.

(1) Students' Self-Confidence Sub-Scale

In the current study, a five-point Likert scale with seven items was used to measure the degree of EFL students' self-confidence in believing in their learning success. The sub-scale was developed by Greene et al. (2004). Some items were slightly modified to be anchored to the EFL learning context (e. g. , "Compared to others in this class, I think I am good at learning English."). Items in the sub-scale scored from 1 (totally disagree) to 5 (totally agree). Adequate internal consistency reliability was reported for the confidence scale ($\alpha = 0.91$) (Greene et al., 2004). Since the validity of the self-confidence sub-scale has been examined and confirmed in previous studies relating to academic confidence, students' achievement, and learning engagement (Greene & Miller, 1996; Green et al., 2004; Miller et al., 1996), the internal consistency was also proved to be acceptable in the current study ($\alpha = 0.740$).

(2) Language Anxiety Sub-Scale

A subscale of EFL learners' language anxiety was adopted from Papi's (2010) modified scale which was to explore the anxiety level of EFL Learners. There were six original items described by forms of questions. In order to keep consistency with other sub-scales, the current study converted the original items into statement descriptions (e.g.. "I become nervous and confused when I am speaking in my English class") (Zhang et al., 2020). In Papi's study, the Cronbach Alpha internal consistency reliability was 0.67, which showed that reliability was met on those items, and in Zhang et al.'s (2020) study, the internal consistency reliability was also reported ($\alpha = 0.89$). Since this subscale was found to have a good model fit by the CFA test (Zhang et al., 2020), it was adopted as a subscale under students' language learning attitude. In order to keep with the guidelines proposed by Bandura (1995), in the current study, the measure of language anxiety was aligned with the measures of students' self-confidence to achieve the same level of specificity. Items in the sub-scale scored from 1 (never) to 5 (always). The Cronbach α internal consistency reliability of the present study was 0.877.

3) Listening Proficiency Test

In the current study, changes in Chinese EFL students' listening proficiency were analyzed using a pretest-posttest design. "Pretest-posttest designs are widely used in behavioral research, primarily for the purpose of comparing groups and or measuring change resulting from experimental treatment" (Dimitrov & Rumrill, 2003, p. 159).

He also proposed that a pretest-posttest design could improve internal validity (Dimitrov & Rumrill, 2003). The internal validity of the present design was strong as the pre-stest of students' listening proficiency ensured that the three experimental groups were equal in their listening proficiency before treatment.

In this study, the listening part of the College English Test Band 4 (CET-4) was chosen as the pre-test and post-test to determine the effects of teacher support on students' English listening proficiency. Aiming at improving English teaching at Chinese universities and measuring Chinese undergraduates' level of English proficiency objectively and accurately, the CET test has been conducted as a standardized examination by the National Education Examination Authority of China (nd). As an official English test, the CET has a crucial effect on Chinese university students' graduation and future employment. According to Jia and Yue (2019), most job seekers in China are required to prove their English proficiency through CET certificates and their first basic salary greatly depends on whether they got a CET certificate.

All participants were enrolled in a 17-week course. They took the pre-test at the first week and then began the study on the blended course from week 2 to week 16. The post-test was administered in week 17. The test involved 30-minutes of listening with 25 multiple-choice questions. In this listening test, three parts are involved. The first part includes three short news with 7 question items; the second part includes two long conversations with 8 question items; the last part contains three passages with 10 question items. Students will listen to each audio only once. They need to catch the question for each item and then choose the best answer from the four choices. The full mark of each item is 7.1 credit in the first 15 items and each of the rest 10 items is 14.2 credits. Because the listening test is only a part of the CET, the full score in the listening test is 248.5 which accounts for 35% of the total CET score of 710. The passing score in this listening test is 149.

6. Data Analysis

This part presents how data was collected and analyzed to the three research questions posed in Chapter I of the present study. SPSS 23.0 software was used to analyze the collected data on students' learning engagement, language learning attitude, and listening proficiency.

1) Analysis of Students' Learning Engagement Survey

In this study, participants were given different types of teacher support, which were teacher's emotional support, cognitive support and autonomy support. Descriptive analysis, one-way ANOVA, and paired sample t-tests were conducted in the pre-survey and post-survey to examine the changes in the level of students' behavioral engagement, cognitive engagement, and emotional engagement before and after the treatment. Descriptive analyses were conducted to both pre-survey and post-survey, which could provide the mean value of different factors and the total scale on students' learning engagement. Paired sample t-test was conducted to examine the changes in participants' learning engagement before and after treatment under the influence of different types of teacher support. One-way ANOVA was also conducted in the post-survey to examine the group difference in students' engagement as a result of different types of teacher support. The P values were set at 0.05.

2) Analysis of Students' Language Learning Attitude Survey

For the students' language learning attitude survey, descriptive statistics, paired sample t-test and one-way ANOVA were performed to investigate the changes in students' attitude on language learning in terms of self-confidence and language anxiety before and after the experiment and whether there was any difference on students' language learning attitude among different groups under a blended learning environment.

3) Analysis of Students' Listening Proficiency Test Score

To examine the effect of different types of teacher support on students' learning engagement and language learning attitude before and after treatment, descriptive analysis and paired sample t-test were adopted. Then one-way analysis of variances (ANOVA) was conducted on the collected data to explore the difference between different types of teacher support in affecting students' learning engagement and language learning attitude.

Table 3-10 Summary of Research Questions, Data Dollection, and Data Analysis

Research questions	Data collection	Data analysis
1. Effects of teacher support on Chinese EFL students' learning engagement in a blended learning environment	Pre-survey Post-survey	Descriptive statistics Paired sample *t* -test One-way ANOVA
2. Effects of teacher support on Chinese EFL students' learning attitude in a blended learning environment	Pre-survey Post-survey	Descriptive statistics Paired sample *t* -test One-way ANOVA
3. Effects of teacher support on Chinese EFL students' listening proficiency in a blended learning environment	Proficiency test Pre-test Post-test	Descriptive statistics Paired sample *t* -test One-way ANOVA

The effect of teacher support on students' listening proficiency in the pre-test and post-test were analyzed using descriptive analysis, paired sample t-tests, and one-way ANOVA analysis. Paired t-tests were employed to compare the improvements in participants' listening proficiency before and after the treatment. One-way ANOVA was adopted to determine whether there were differential effects of teacher support on participants' listening proficiency. Bonferroni post hoc tests were also used to determine which group achieved a better effect than the other. The post hoc test was used to determine where differences lay among groups.

第四章 结果及讨论

基于实施的分组教学活动，本章将对学生的测试前、后调查问卷及听力测试的结果进行分析，从而探讨在混合式学习环境下，教师的情感支持、认知支持和自主支持三种不同类型的支持行为对EFL学生在学习投入、语言学习态度和听力水平三方面的影响。本章第一部分分析了在相同的混合学习环境下，不同类型的教师支持对学生学习投入（行为投入、认知投入和情感投入）的影响；第二部分分析了不同类型的教师支持对学生的语言学习态度产生的影响（包括自信心和语言焦虑两部分）；第三部分则分析探讨了混合学习环境下，不同类型的教师支持对学习者英语听力水平的影响。

Chapter 4 Results and Discussion

The present study explores the effects of three different types of teacher support (emotional support, cognitive support, and autonomy support) on Chinese EFL students' learning engagement, language learning attitude and English listening proficiency under a blended learning environment. The first part of this chapter provides the effects of different types of teacher support on participants' learning engagement, namely, behavioral engagement, cognitive engagement and emotional engagement, under the same blended learning environment. The second part shows the effects of different types of teacher support on participants' language learning attitude in terms of confidence and language anxiety in a blended learning environment. The third part reports the effects of different types of teacher support on participants' listening proficiency in a blended learning environment.

1. Effects of Teacher Support on EFL Students' Learning Engagement in a Blended Learning Environment

1) Changes in EFL Students' Learning Engagement

In order to investigate the level of learning engagement of all participants before they started to learn the blended course, a pre-survey on EFL students' learning engagement level was conducted. A descriptive analysis was used to analyze the mean level of learning engagement of all participants. Since the pre-treatment engagement difference between the groups is not the focus of the current study, only the mean level of learning engagement for all participants will be discussed.

Considering students' learning engagement contains three dimensions with six factors, the total engagement level in the pre-survey will be reported and discussed from different dimensions and factors. As presented in Table 4-1, it shows that the total average level of engagement of all participants was 3.28. Although it was a little higher than the middle level of 3.00 in the theoretical mean, it did not mean a strong level on EFL students' engagement in blended learning.

Table 4-1 Descriptive Statistics of the Pre-survey of Students' Total Engagement

Dimension	Factor	N	*M*	*SD*	*M*	*SD*
Behavioral Engagement	Group work	66	3.34	0.55	3.63	0.76
	Teacher-student interaction				3.02	0.75
	Active learning				3.59	0.78
Cognitive Engagement	Implementing learning strategy	66	3.14	0.58	3.09	0.69
	Self-regulation				3.23	0.63
Emotional Engagement	Emotional involvement	66	3.41	0.68	3.41	0.68
Valid N		66	3.28			

Regarding the three dimensions of learning engagement, the mean ranked from high to low were: emotional engagement, behavioral engagement, and cognitive engagement. In the current study, the emotional engagement dimension has only one factor with 5 items. The mean of emotional engagement was at a relatively higher level ($M = 3.41$), which had achieved the theoretical mean. In terms of behavioral engagement, the total mean was 3.34. In specific, under behavioral engagement, students' engagement in group work was the highest with a mean value of 3.63, and teacher-student interaction was the lowest with a mean value of 3.02, which indicated that participants in the current study were not as engaged in the interaction with their teachers.

On the contrary, regarding the overall level of cognitive engagement of all participants in the pre-survey, the total mean was 3.14. Under cognitive engagement, the mean value in self-regulation and implementing learning strategy did not show a high theoretical level, with a mean score of 3.09 in implementing learning strategy and 3.23 in self-regulation, indicating that the participants did not often apply learning strategy in their blended language learning and lacked self-regulation during blended learning. It might be due to teachers' neglect of the importance of strategy instruction. Another reason for these situations might be that participants seldom made a learning plan in blended learning and they usually did not integrate the language knowledge with other knowledge or course.

The pre-survey was a reflection of how much the participants had been involved in their blended learning before the experimental course. Regarding the results of the participants' total engagement in the three different dimensions, their emotional engagement ranks the highest, followed by behavioral engagement. Participants' engagement level in each factor showed that students had a relevant lower engagement in the interaction with their teachers and did not put much effort in self-regulation and applying learning strategies in their past blended learning experience. These results were similar to the data in Ma and Zhou's (2019) study which concluded that students' emotional engagement was higher than cognitive and behavioral engagement in a blended learning environment. This indicated that the blended learning environment that students experienced enabled them to have more chances to communicate and cooperate with their teachers and peers, making students more interested and focused on their course (Ma & Zhou, 2019).

To explore the answer to the question that whether there are any effects of different types of teacher support on EFL students' learning engagement in a blended learning environment, a comparison between pre-survey and post-survey learning engagement was implemented to all participants. Because students' learning engagement is a multifaceted construct with three dimensions and six factors in the current study, descriptive statistics and paired sample t-tests were conducted on the pre-survey and post-survey on students' learning engagement in terms of dimensional level and total level.

In order to explore what changes happened to participants' learning engagement on the dimensional level with different types of support provided by their teacher, paired sample t-tests were firstly applied on students' behavioral engagement, cognitive engagement, and emotional engagement to each group between their pre-survey and post-survey. As shown in Table 4-2, for the emotional support group, participants in this group showed statistically significant improvement in their behavioral, cognitive, and emotional engagement between the pre-survey and post-survey as the p values are all lower than 0.05 ($p < 0.05$). For instance, the mean level of behavioral engagement in the emotional support group increased from 3.37 in the pre-survey to 3.47 in the post-survey, with a significant improvement in their behavioral engagement after the experiment ($p = 0.001$). The improvement of participants' cognitive engagement also changed from 3.12 in the pre-survey to 3.18 in the post-survey, indicating a significant improvement after treatment ($p = 0.016$). Moreover, participants' emotional engagement improved from 3.27 in the pre-survey to 3.41 in the post-survey, which meant that EFL students' emotional engagement can be effectively improved by the emotional support from their teachers in a blended learning environment ($p = 0.010$). The results in the emotional support group showed that EFL students' behavioral engagement, cognitive engagement, and emotional engagement can be effectively improved by teachers' emotional support.

Table 4-2 Changes in Students' Learning Engagement according to Teacher Support Types

Group	Learning Engagement	Pre-Survey		Post-Survey		t	p
		M	SD	M	SD		
ES	Behavioral Engagement	3.37	0.56	3.47	0.50	3.701	0.001**
	Cognitive Engagement	3.12	0.53	3.18	0.47	2.627	0.016**
	Emotional Engagement	3.27	0.67	3.41	0.62	2.832	0.010**

续表

Group	Learning Engagement	Pre-Survey		Post-Survey		t	p
		M	SD	M	SD		
CS	Behavioral Engagement	3.20	0.59	3.29	0.57	3.501	0.002**
	Cognitive Engagement	3.07	0.74	3.78	0.48	7.961	0.000***
	Emotional Engagement	3.44	0.68	3.32	0.68	2.017	0.057
AS	Behavioral Engagement	3.43	0.51	3.84	0.43	12.564	0.000***
	Cognitive Engagement	3.22	0.47	3.37	0.43	3.128	0.005**
	Emotional Engagement	3.67	0.65	3.72	0.64	2.017	0.057

*$p < 0.05$, **$p < 0.01$, ***$p < 0.001$; ES: Emotional support group, CS: Cognitive support group, AS: Autonomy support group

Regarding the improvement in the cognitive support group, participants' behavioral engagement changed positively from 3.20 in the pre-survey to 3.29 in the post-survey. There was a significant improvement in their behavioral engagement ($p = 0.002$), which indicated that EFL students' behavioral engagement could be effectively influenced by teacher's cognitive support in a blended learning environment. As for the improvement in participants' cognitive engagement, it showed that the mean score increased significantly from 3.07 in the pre-survey to 3.78 in the post-survey. The improvement in their cognitive engagement was statistically significant ($p = 0.000$). It revealed that EFL students' cognitive engagement could be greatly improved under the influence of teacher's cognitive support. Surprisingly, the mean score in participants' emotional engagement was 3.44 in the pre-survey while reduced to 3.32 in the post-survey. There was even no improvement in students' emotional engagement ($p = 0.057$), indicating that cognitive support could not significantly improve

EFL students' emotional engagement under a blended learning environment. That is, teacher's cognitive support could significantly improve EFL students' behavioral engagement and cognitive engagement.

As for the autonomy support group, participants' behavioral engagement was enhanced from 3.43 in the pre-survey to 3.84 in the post-survey. There was a statistically significant improvement in their behavioral engagement between the pre-survey and post-survey (p = 0.000). It revealed that autonomy support could effectively facilitate the improvement of EFL students' behavioral engagement. Moreover, the mean score of participants' cognitive engagement was 3.22 in the pre-survey and 3.37 in the post-survey. The significant improvement had been achieved after the experiment (p = 0.005), which meant that teacher autonomy support can also positively improve EFL students' cognitive engagement. Interestingly, participants' emotional engagement did not show significant improvement between the pre-survey and post-survey (p = 0.057), with a mean score of 3.67 in the pre-survey and 3.72 in the post-survey. It could be inferred that teacher autonomy support does not have a significant effect in improving students' emotional engagement. In general, EFL students could benefit from teacher autonomy support in improving their behavioral engagement and cognitive engagement in a blended learning environment.

Considering the results of t-tests on EFL students' learning engagement between pre-survey and post-survey, teacher's emotional support could effectively improve EFL students' behavioral engagement, cognitive engagement, and emotional engagement. As harmonious relationships between teachers and students are regarded as the premise and guarantee for the realization of learning effect. The findings were consistent with the study of Ruzek et al. (2016) who found that teacher's emotional support could promote students' active learning behavior and academic achievement. In addition, some scholars also discovered that teacher's emotional support played a more significant role in the learning process than people imagined, which had been confirmed in Pianta et al.'s (2008) study whichfound that teacher's emotional support might have a greater impact on students' performance than teaching quality.

Based on SDT, teacher's emotional support is important for individuals because it is an external resource related to individuals' personal needs, which stated that healthy development in students' psychology requires a harmonious and caring external environment. Under the learning context, it was conducive to establishing students' sense of belonging when they perceived love and respects from their teachers, which may consequently formulate students' internal learning motivation (Niemiec & Ryan, 2009). What's more, Ryan and Deci (2000) pointed out that students are more willing to accept values in class when they perceive the teacher's respect and care. Therefore, providing teacher's emotional support can be a starting point when introducing relevant learning concepts to students. Emotional support can also effectively buffer the negative effects of negative events and emotions, thus eliminating the obstacles to students' learning engagement (Sakiz et al., 2012). In addition, in Sakiz et al.'s (2012) study, they found that teacher's emotional support can reduce students' learning helplessness, which is not conducive to improving their learning engagement. Moreover, a similar result was also confirmed by Way et al.'s (2007) study. In brief, teacher's emotional support can significantly promote EFL student's learning engagement under a blended learning environment.

In terms of teacher's cognitive support, the results of t-tests in the current study demonstrated that teacher's cognitive support has significant effects in enhancing students' behavioral engagement and cognitive engagement. The findings have been confirmed in previous research (Hospel &Galand, 2016; Skinner & Belmont, 1993; Wentzel et al., 2016) which all proved that teacher's cognitive support positively influences students' behavioral engagement and cognitive engagement to a different extent. Conveying expectations to students, providing appropriate learning tools and strategies, supplying appropriate guidance and help, and providing cognition-related or competence-related feedback are essential teacher behaviors to achieve effective teaching results, and they are also the essence of the teachers' role (Kersey & Spray, 2016; Reeve & Jang, 2006; Jang et al., 2010).

Under the conceptual framework of SDT, teacher's cognitive support can promote the satisfaction of students' needs in competence (Legault et al., 2006). Satisfaction to the need for competence is the most direct leading factor to students' behavioral engagement, which confirmed the findings in the current study that students' behavioral engagement had been significantly improved under the influence of teacher's cognitive support in a blended learning environment. The significant effect indicated that EFL students' needs for competence had been well satisfied with the influence of teacher's cognitive support. This is because only when competence needs are satisfied, students are likely to make efforts to try and cope with academic challenges (Legault et al., 2006). As Ryan and Deci (2009) pointed out, the satisfaction of students' competence needs is also considered as the basis of learning motivation. They also regarded that positive feedback from teachers under cognitive support can enhance students' sense of competence and further promote the formation of individual intrinsic motivation.

Furthermore, findings of the current study also confirmed the previous studies that teacher's cognitively supportive behavior was associated with students' high application of learning strategy (Yildirim, 2012), higher self-regulation (Patrick et al., 2007), and positive interpersonal behavior (Battistich et al., 1997). Henderlong and Lepper (2002) also mentioned that when students perceived the feedback as sincere and focused on improving their abilities rather than comparing with others, teacher feedback in cognitive support has a more significant effect on students' intrinsic motivation, which would promote students to more engage in learning. However, the current study found that teacher's cognitive support cannot significantly promote students' emotional engagement during the learning process.

Findings in the current study showed that teacher autonomy support is effective in improving EFL students' behavioral engagement and cognitive engagement. The findings echoed to the conclusions of previous studies that the more teacher's autonomy support during the teaching process, the more effort students will engage in their learning (Assor et al., 2002; Greene et al., 2004; Hospel & Galand, 2016; Reeve et al., 2004). Specifically, teacher's autonomy support could facilitate students to pay more effort to their academic learning, perceive positive academic emotion, be more persistent when facing difficulties, and more frequently apply cognitive and meta-cognitive strategies during the learning process.

Compared to their primary and middle school periods, students who enter university possess more freedom. At the same time, they have more demands on their autonomy than before. As Roeser et al. (2000) said that students' development requires opportunities in autonomous choice and self-determination. In addition, students who perceive more autonomy will have more desire to learn and engage more autonomously in their studies (Deci et al., 1981). Finding in the current study supports the view in SDT that ideal learning engagement can be a product of students' autonomy motivation, which could be greatly stimulated out under an autonomous supportive environment (Reeve, 2012). Compared to students who are taught under a controlling style, students who perceive autonomy support from their teachers are more likely to demonstrate impressive learning outcomes, such as student engagement (Jang et al., 2010). In the current study, teacher's autonomy support enhanced students' sense of self-determination and psychological freedom, thus making students more engaged in learning activities.

However, the current study found that EFL students did not gain significant improvement in their emotional engagement with the help of teacher autonomy support. A similar finding was also confirmed by Yuan and Kim (2017) that autonomy support seemed to have contributed to participants' emotional engagement, whereas, there was no statistically significant difference. Since the effects of different types of teacher support on different dimensions of learning engagement have been discussed and partly confirmed, in order to explore changes in the total engagement level in different groups, paired sample t-test was conducted again on the total level.

Interestingly, different from the result in the dimensional level, each type of teacher support performed significant effects in enhancing EFL students' total engagement level (See Table 4-3). To be specific, in the emotional support group, participants' total engagement level scored 3.27 in the pre-survey while 3.36 in the post-survey. The t-test results showed statistically significant mean differences between the pre-survey and post-survey mean scores ($t = 4.516$, $p = 0.000$). The mean score of the cognitive group was 3.17 on the pre-survey and 3.46 on the post-survey. The findings presented a statistically significant difference between the pre-survey and the post-survey ($t = 7.663$, $p = 0.000$), indicating the improvement of participants' learning engagement as an effect of teacher's cognitive support with EFL students. Participants' mean score on the pre-survey in the autonomy support group was 3.41 and increased to 3.66 on the post-survey. The findings also showed a statistically significant difference between the mean score on the pre-survey and the post-survey ($t = 9.574$, $p = 0.000$).

Table 4-3 Changes in Students' Total Engagement in Groups under Teacher Support

Group	Learning Engagement				t	p
	Pre-Survey		Post-Survey			
	M	SD	M	SD		
ES ($n = 22$)	3.27	0.50	3.36	0.44	4.516	0.000***
CS ($n = 22$)	3.17	0.50	3.46	0.43	7.663	0.000***
AS ($n = 22$)	3.41	0.36	3.66	0.30	9.574	0.000***

* $p < 0.05$, ** $p < 0.01$, *** $p < 0.001$

Participants in all three groups achieved statistically significant improvement in their learning engagement. The findings suggest that different teacher support in all experimental groups results in improvement of EFL students' learning engagement. In addition, the significant improvement in students' learning engagement under each type of teacher support also showed that with one kind of engagement being improved, other kinds of learning engagement will be enhanced at the same time.

As for teacher's emotional support, findings in the current study revealed that teacher's emotional support is also effective to EFL students' positive learning engagement. This has been confirmed in the previous studies which stated that teacher's emotional support is essential to students' motivation and engagement (Cooper, 2013; Eccles & Wang, 2014). A similar statement was also shown that when students feel emotionally supported by their teacher, they turn to engage more fully in their academic learning (Goodenow, 1993; Wentzel, 1994). When teachers provide care and concerns to students, it would encourage students' engagement in school and desire to achieve the teacher's expectations and wishes (Patrick, et al., 2007). The findings were also in accordance with Lam et al.'s (2012) study with Hong Kong junior secondary school students which suggested that students became more engaged in their behavior, cognition and emotion in their study when they perceived teachers to provide emotional support.

When comes to teacher's cognitive support, results in the paired sample t-test indicated that teacher's cognitive support in English learning could facilitate EFL students' overall learning engagement.

The findings were also asserted by Sha et al. (2020) thatstudents' demonstrated significant improvement in their learning engagement with teacher's cognitive support in a blended learning environment. Since the development of university students' thinking is in the reality-oriented practical stage, flexible thinking begins to appear at this stage, that is, they want to learn new strategies in analyzing and solving problems. Therefore, when teachers provide cognitive support to university EFL students, their learning engagement, especially cognitive engagement will also change significantly.

With a view to teacher autonomy support, the effects have been demonstrated in the autonomy support group, indicating that teacher autonomy support is important and effective in improving EFL students' overall learning engagement. This is in line with teachers who teach in an autonomy-supportive style that could improve learners' self-autonomy and then enhance their autonomy, which finally promote students' learning engagement (Jang et al., 2010). Similarly, Dincer et al. (2012) also asserted that perceived autonomy support could positively predict EFL students' learning engagement. When teachers created and provided an autonomy-supportive classroom context, EFL students mostly participated in the course activities and felt more confident in their language competence.

Overall, by comparing the total engagement level and different dimensional engagement levels under the influence of different types of teacher support in the pre-survey and post-survey, findings showed that from the total improvement in learning engagement level, all types of teacher support have a positive role in improving EFL students' learning engagement, which is a similar conclusion made by Chong et al.

(2015) who noted that teacher support plays an independent contribution to students' behavioral, cognitive, and emotional engagement. It was also in accordance with the previous studies which asserted that students' perceived teacher support has been proved to significantly influence students' engagement in terms of behavioral engagement, emotional engagement, and cognitive engagement in both a face-to-face classroom context (Fredricks et al., 2004) and an online context (Liu et al., 2017). It was also stated that teachers could apply instructional strategies and supportive behaviors to improve EFL students' engagement (Mercer & Dörnyei, 2020). Therefore, they can provide different types of support to establish a supportive environment with constructive teacher-student interactions, which can improve students' learning engagement (Parsons et al., 2014; Skinner et al., 2008).

From different engagement dimensions, teacher's emotional support has a significant effect in improving EFL students' behavioral engagement, cognitive engagement, and emotional engagement. Teacher's cognitive support has a significant impact in enhancing EFL students' behavioral engagement and cognitive engagement. Moreover, teacher's autonomy support is effective in promoting EFL students' behavioral engagement and cognitive engagement in a blended learning environment.

2) *Group Difference in EFL Students' Learning Engagement*

As participants were divided into three groups according to different types of teacher support given, the significant improvement in EFL students' learning engagement in different dimensions was almost confirmed. To investigate whether there was any significant group difference in different dimensions of learning engagement, one-way ANOVA analysis was firstly conducted to the pre-survey mean scores among the three experimental groups to examine homogeneity of variance.

Table 4-4 Test of Homogeneity of Variances on Different Engagement in the Pre-Survey

Engagement	Levene Statistic	*df*1	*df*2	*Sig.*
Behavioral	0.841	2	63	0.436
Cognitive	1.609	2	63	0.208
Emotional	0.049	2	63	0.953

In Table 4-4, the result of the Levene Statistic test in behavioral engagement was 0.841 and the significance value was 0.436. Similarly, the result of the Levene Statistic test in cognitive engagement was 1.609 with a significance value of 0.208. Regarding emotional engagement, the result of Levene Statistic test in pre-survey was 0.049 and the significance value was 0.953. All the results indicated that the variance between groups was equal($p > 0.05$).

Table 4-5 One-Way ANOVA for Total Learning Engagement Pre-Survey

Engagement		Sum of Squares	*df*	Mean Square	*F*	*p*
Behavioral	Between Groups	0.642	2	0.321	1.051	0.356
	Within Groups	19.245	63	0.380		
	Total	19.887	65			

续表

Engagement		Sum of Squares	*df*	Mean Square	*F*	*p*
Cognitive	Between Groups	0.265	2	0.133	0.380	0.685
	Within Groups	21.984	63	0.349		
	Total	22.249	65			
Emotional	Between Groups	2.347	2	1.173	2.658	0.078
	Within Groups	27.811	63	0.441		
	Total	30.158	65			

$*p < 0.05$, $**p < 0.01$, $***p < 0.001$

As shown in Table 4-5 above, as the p value in behavioral engagement, cognitive engagement and emotional engagement were all over 0.05 in ANOVA, it showed that there was no statistically significant difference between groups on different types of engagement in the pre-survey, which indicated that the three types of learning engagement level of all participants turned out to be homogeneous before the treatment.

In order to investigate whether there was any difference in the improvement on EFL students' different types of learning engagement among different groups, one-way ANOVA was again employed to explore the answer. The variance significance of homogeneity of variances on the improvement in post-survey were all over 0.05 ($p > 0.05$), indicating equal variance was assumed in behavioral engagement, cognitive engagement, and emotional engagement.

Table 4-6　One-Way ANOVA on Different Learning Engagement in Post-Survey

Engagement		Sum of Squares	*df*	Mean Square	*F*	*p*
Behavioral	Between Groups	3.526	2	1.763	7.025	0.002**
	Within Groups	15.810	63	0.251		
	Total	19.336	65			
Cognitive	Between Groups	4.163	2	2.081	9.773	0.000***
	Within Groups	13.418	63	0.213		
	Total	17.580	65			
Emotional	Between Groups	1.935	2	0.967	2.310	0.108
	Within Groups	26.384	63	0.419		
	Total	28.318	65			

* $p < 0.05$, ** $p < 0.01$, *** $p < 0.001$

The result of ANOVA in Table 4-6 showed a statistically significant difference in behavioral engagement among the three groups in the post-survey ($F = 7.025$, $p = 0.002$). That is, the effects of teacher support on EFL students' behavioral engagement were statistically different among groups according to the types of teacher support given. In addition, there was also a statistically significant in cognitive engagement among the three groups in the post-survey ($F = 9.773$, $p = 0.000$). Whereas, on emotional engagement, there was no significant difference among groups in the post-survey. Therefore, in order to explore the significant group difference in students' behavioral engagement and cognitive engagement, Bonferroni post hoc tests were conducted to examine the significant differences among groups.

As shown in Table 4-7, in terms of participants' behavioral engagement, the results of the Bonferroni post hoc test showed that there was a significant difference in the mean difference between the autonomy support group and the cognitive support group (MD $=0.56$, $p=0.001$). The results indicated that autonomy support could promote EFL students' behavioral engagement more significantly than cognitive support in a blended learning environment.

Table 4-7 Results of Bonferroni Post Hoc Test for Improvement in Learning Engagement

Post-Survey	Groups	*MD*	*SE*	*p*
Behavioral Engagement	AS > CS	0.56	0.15	0.001**
	AS > ES	0.37	0.15	0.051
	ES > CS	0.18	0.15	0.673
Cognitive Engagement	CS > ES	0.56	0.60	0.000***
	CS > AS	0.41	0.14	0.012**
	AS > ES	0.19	0.14	0.552

$* p<0.05$, $** p<0.01$, $*** p<0.001$

Surprisingly, no statistically significant difference was found between the autonomy support group and the emotional support group (MD $=0.37$, $p=0.051$), indicating that autonomy support and cognitive support have the same effects in improving EFL students' learning engagement in a blended learning environment. Similarly, there was no significant difference between cognitive support group and emotional support group (MD $=0.18$, $p=0.673$). It meant that teacher's cognitive support and emotional support are equally effective in promoting students' behavioral engagement under a blended learning environment. Therefore, the findings showed that teacher's autonomy support is more beneficial for EFL students to promote their behavioral engagement. And different types of teacher support do not perform significant differences in improving EFL students' behavioral engagement in a blended learning environment.

In terms of participants' cognitive engagement, there was a significant mean difference between the cognitive support group and the emotional support group (MD = 0.56, p = 0.000), indicating that cognitive support is more significantly effective than emotional support in enhancing EFL students' cognitive engagement under a blended learning environment. Moreover, a significant mean difference was also shown between the cognitive support group and the autonomy support group (MD = 0.41, p = 0.012), which symbolized that teacher's cognitive support is more beneficial for EFL students to improve their cognitive engagement than autonomy support.

However, there was no significant difference in the improvement of students' cognitive engagement between the autonomy support group and the emotional support group (MD = 0.19, p = 0.552). That is, there is no difference between teacher autonomy support and emotional support in promoting EFL students' cognitive engagement in a blended learning environment. Therefore, cognitive support was more beneficial for EFL students in improving their cognitive engagement under a blended learning environment. Moreover, teacher's cognitive support is also superior to their autonomy support in encouraging EFL students' cognitive engagement. No significant difference between teacher's autonomy support and emotional support in improving students' cognitive engagement.

Overall, in terms of EFL students' behavioral engagement, findings showed that autonomy support is more beneficial for EFL students to enhance their level of behavioral engagement compared to cognitive support. There is no significant difference between autonomy support and emotional support, and between cognitive support and emotional support in improving EFL students' behavioral engagement.

According to the previous research, students' learning engagement is closely related to teacher's autonomy support (Wei et al., 2020). Findings in the current study lent support to the study of Jang et al. (2010) who investigated students from nine public high schools and found that if teachers were perceived as providing autonomy support in class, students would be found to perform at a higher level of collective behavioral engagement. In addition, the current findings also asserted the conclusion made by Yoo (2015), which stated that teacher autonomy support was positively correlated with students' autonomous motivation and behavioral engagement in PE class. The positive relationship between autonomy support and behavioral engagement can be explained by the increase of autonomic motivation, that is, an autonomy-supportive environment could enhance students' internal sense of autonomy, thus improving students' autonomic motivation, which consequently makes students show more engagement in their learning behaviors. In brief, the autonomous support environment provided by teachers is a necessary condition for increasing students' autonomous motivation and behavioral engagement in class (Hagger, et al., 2005). Hein (2016) also confirmed the effect of autonomy support on students' behavioral engagement. He emphasized that when students perceive teacher's autonomy support, it could fulfill students' needs for autonomy. Similarly, according to Meyer and Turner (2006), students' learning engagement requires the consistently positive emotional experience provided by teacher's autonomy support, which may closely connect teacher's autonomy support with students' behavioral engagement.

In terms of EFL students' cognitive engagement, the current study found that EFL students benefit more by given cognitive support than they did by given emotional support and autonomy support. However, teacher autonomy support and emotional support play a similar effect in improving EFL students' cognitive engagement under a blended learning environment.

However, different from the current study, Wang and Eccles (2015) stated in their study that teacher cognitive support directly predicate students' behavioral engagement and emotional engagement, which was in conflict with the current study. The reason for this might be that the definition of cognitive support is broader than in their study. In the current study, except for teachers providing the importance of knowledge and affording linking with their study to their real-life, it also provides supports in how to use different strategies in language learning and how to connect the strategies with other skills they have learned before. Meanwhile, participants in the cognitive support group were providing more sufficient learning resources and materials in a blended learning environment. Considering all this, it is possible for students to improve their cognitive engagement significantly than other types of teacher support.

The current study lent support to Guthrie et al.'s (2004) study that students who were provided with strategy support tend to have and apply more cognitive strategies during their reading process and students who were with more cognitive support were more motivated than students who did not. Since teacher cognitive support has also been considered as competence support or structure support. The results of the current study confirmed the previous study of Luo (2017) that teacher's learning-focused cognitive support may positively predict students' cognitive engagement related to metacognitive self-regulation. It was believed that when teachers provide learning-focused cognitive support, they may emphasize learning and improvement, and they may pay more attention to students' needs and resources in motivation. They may also support students understanding the learning topic by linking it with their real-life experience, which in turn stimulates students' cognitive engagement.

In terms of EFL students' emotional engagement, findings indicated that all types of teacher support could have a similar effect in improving students' emotional engagement in a blended learning environment. There is no significant difference in the improvement of students' emotional engagement when teacher's emotional support, cognitive support, and autonomy support are given respectively. These findings were in accordance with Liu et al.'s (2017) study which found that teacher's emotional, cognitive, and autonomy support all contributed to students' emotional engagement. Ryan and Patric (2001), Sadoughi and Hejazi (2021), and Tas et al. (2019) also confirmed the current finding that three types of teacher support are all effective in improving students' emotional engagement, but there was no significant difference between them.

2. Effects of Teacher Support on EFL Students' Language Learning Attitude in a Blended Learning Environment

1) Changes in EFL Students' Language Learning Attitude

Another purpose of the current study was to investigate the changes in EFL students' learning attitude towards language learning in terms of self-confidence and language anxiety under the influence of different types of teacher support. Paired sample t-tests were used to answer this question. Comparisons across the three experimental groups on the mean scores of the pre-survey and post-survey were conducted. Table 4-8 demonstrated the results of descriptive statistics and paired sample t-tests in EFL students' self-confidence in language learning and language anxiety.

By viewing the results in the paired sample t-test, changes in three groups all showed participants' positive responses in their self-confidence to different types of teacher support. Moreover, the results in language anxiety also performed significant negative responses to different types of teacher support. Regarding EFL students' self-confidence in language learning, all three experimental groups performed significantly improvement in the post-survey than they did in the pre-survey.

Table 4-8 Changes in EFL Students' Language Learning Attitude to Different Teacher Support

Dimension	Group	Pre-survey		Post-survey		t	p
		M	SD	M	SD		
Self-Confidence	ES	2.94	0.44	3.16	0.43	3.930	0.001**
	CS	3.15	0.49	3.38	0.25	2.136	0.045*
	AS	3.18	0.36	3.66	0.33	5.768	0.000***
Language anxiety	ES	3.38	0.46	2.74	0.37	6.345	0.000***
	CS	3.51	0.34	3.06	0.28	5.742	0.000***
	AS	3.40	0.42	2.98	0.32	5.919	0.000***

* $p < 0.05$, ** $p < 0.01$, *** $p < 0.001$

Specifically, the mean score in the emotional support group was 2.94 in the pre-survey and turned out to be 3.16 in the post-survey, indicating a significant improvement in participant' self-confidence when emotional support was given ($t = 3.930$, $p = 0.001$). In addition, the mean score of learning confidence of cognitive support in the pre-survey changed from 3.15 to 3.38 in the post-survey, which revealed that EFL students could improve their self-confidence with the cognitive support from their teachers ($t = 2.136$, $p = 0.045$). Moreover, participants' self-confidence in language learning was enhanced from 3.18 in the pre-survey to 3.66 in the post-survey by giving autonomy support. That is, autonomy support can also promote EFL students' self-confidence in language learning ($t = 5.768$, $p = 0.000$).

In terms of EFL students' learning attitude changed in language anxiety, the mean scores all responded negatively to different types of teacher support. Different from learning confidence in the attitude survey, the scores on the post-survey of students' language anxiety turned out to reduce than the pre-survey. The reason for this is because of the score setting in the language anxiety sub-scale that the higher the score, the more anxiety students perceive, vice versa, the lower the score, the less anxiety they feel. That is, there is a negative relationship between teacher support and language anxiety.

In specific, participants' language anxiety in the emotional support group changed from 3.38 in the pre-survey to 2.74 in the post-survey, which indicated that teacher's emotional support can significantly help EFL students to reduce their language learning anxiety ($t = 6.345$, $p = 0.000$). While the mean score of language anxiety in the cognitive support group reduced from 3.51 in the pre-survey to 3.06 in post-survey, indicating that cognitive support may also significantly reduce EFL students' language anxiety ($t = 5.742$, $p = 0.000$). Moreover, in the autonomy support group, the mean score on participants' language anxiety decreased from 3.40 in pre-survey to 2.98 in post-survey. That is, teacher autonomy support could significantly relax EFL students' anxiety in the language learning process ($t = 5.919$, $p = 0.000$).

Findings in the current study showed that all types of teacher support have a positive effect in enhancing EFL students' self-confidence in language learning. It was consistent with Chang and Bangsri (2020), in which teacher support was believed to increase students' confidence that in turn improve their language proficiency. Because when students perceive supports from their teachers, their self-confidence can be increased (Fong & Krause, 2014). In addition, Sun et al. (2021) also stated that teacher's emotional support, cognitive support, and learning support positively predict students' self-confidence. The findings also support Lorsbach and Jinks's (1999) study which argued that self-confidence depends on personal relationships, in which, students' self-confidence is affected by the relationship with their teachers or classmates. That is, students' self-confidence may be influenced by their teacher's social-comparative appraisals as well as other supportive behaviors. In the current study, although the supports provided to EFL students were different, they all positively influence students' self-confidence in language learning. Similarly, Olani et al. (2010) also confirmed the current study by suggesting that students' self-confidence can not only positively predict learning achievement, which is also closely related to teacher support. In addition, results of the current study were consistent with Fallah's (2013) study which stated that self-confidence and anxiety are two factors closely relate to each other and greatly influence the effects in language learning.

In terms of language anxiety, the findings in the current study also revealed that all types of teacher support can help EFL students significantly ease their language learning anxiety in a blended learning environment. The effects of teacher support on EFL students' attitude in language anxiety indicated that teacher support can be viewed as a buffer from the effects of students' negative emotions, such as language anxiety that they have experienced in foreign language learning (Piechurska-Kuciel, 2011). Since language anxiety is a kind of negative emotion in the foreign language learning process (Horwitz et al., 1986), teacher's emotionally supportive behaviors can facilitate students' feeling of ease, security, and comfort. As for cognitive support, teachers could offer students skills and guidance to help them understand the stressful situations might be produced by the learning process (Liu et al., 2017). Finally, at the level of autonomy support, teachers leave space for students to learn and provide more opportunities for students to develop their own abilities so that students could feel valued and respected by their teachers (Chai & Gong, 2013).

With teacher's emotional support, EFL students' language anxiety had been greatly eased. Since it is believed that "anxiety has both internal and social dimensions" (MacIntyre, 2017, p. 28). Findings in the current study lent support from Palacios's (1998) study which found that perceived teacher support was negatively associated with language anxiety. A similar conclusion was also given by Jin et al. (2015) that teacher support significantly negatively predicted language anxiety among Chinese EFL university students. In the current study, students who were in an emotional-supportive environment could feel more concern, respect, and encouragement during their learning. They can cope with language anxiety better.

As for the autonomy support group, the decrease in EFL students' language anxiety is closely related to their self-confidence. According to Fallah (2013), language anxiety and self-confidence are two closely related factors for that the increase of self-confidence will consequently lead to a decrease in anxiety. Because in the attitude survey related to self-confidence showed that students in the autonomy support group improved significantly with more items, which might be the cause for the reduction in students' language anxiety under the same autonomy-supportive environment.

2) *Group Differences in EFL Students' Language Learning Attitude*

Since participants in all groups demonstrated significant responses to teacher support, the current study also aims at exploring whether there is a group difference in the improvement of EFL students' attitude in terms of their learning confidence and language anxiety under the blended learning environment. In an effort to investigate whether the three experimental groups are homogeneous in their attitude to language learning under the influence of teacher support, one-way ANOVAs were conducted to confirm the significant differences in the pre-survey scores among the three groups. The test of homogeneity of variables showed that equal variance was assumed in both the self-confident and language anxiety pre-survey ($p = 0.532$; $p = 0.310$).

Table 4-9 One-Way ANOVA on Students' Attitudes Toward Language Learning in Pre-Survey

Pre-Survey	ES (n = 22)		CS (n = 22)		AS (n = 22)		F	p
	M	SD	M	SD	M	SD		
Self-Confidence	2.94	0.47	3.15	0.49	3.18	0.36	1.902	0.158
Language Anxiety	3.37	0.46	3.51	0.34	3.40	0.42	0.626	0.538

As shown in Table 4-9, the results of ANOVA identified that the experimental were homogeneous on the mean score in self-confidence ($F = 1.902$, $p = 0.158$), and their language anxiety ($F = 0.626$, $p = 0.538$). There was no significant difference between the pre-survey scores of the current study variables, indicating that the three groups were homogeneous in their self-confidence and language anxiety levels.

Table 4-10 One-Way ANOVA on Students' Language Learning Attitude in Post-Survey

Pre-Survey	ES (n = 22)		CS (n = 22)		AS (n = 22)		F	p
	M	SD	M	SD	M	SD		
Self-Confidence	3.16	0.43	3.38	0.25	3.66	0.33	11.829	0.000***
Language Anxiety	2.73	0.38	3.06	0.28	2.98	0.32	5.852	0.005**

*p < 0.05, **p < 0.01, ***p < 0.001

In order to investigate whether there are differences in EFL students' learning attitude on the post-survey according to different types of teacher support, one-way ANOVAs were conducted between the post-survey mean scores of the three groups. Table 4-10 showed that there was a statistically significant difference in mean score between the three groups in students' self-confidence ($F = 11.829$, $p = 0.000$), and language anxiety ($F = 5.852$, $p = 0.005$). The results indicated that there were significant differences between different types of teacher support on students' language learning attitude in the post-survey. Bonferroni post hoc tests were conducted to explore where the differences appeared among different types of teacher support.

As students' learning attitude under teacher support was explored in terms of two aspects, namely students' self-confidence, and their language anxiety during language learning. From Table 4-11, it can be seen that there were significant group differences in EFL students' attitude change according to different types of teacher support.

Table 4-11 Results of Bonferroni Post Hoc Test on Students' Attitude Toward Language Learning

Dependent Variable	Groups	*MD*	*SE*	*p*
Self-Confidence	AS > ES	0.50	0.10	0.000^{***}
	AS > CS	0.28	0.10	0.026^{*}
	CS > ES	0.22	0.10	0.108
Language Anxiety	ES > CS	0.33	0.10	0.005^{**}
	ES > AS	0.25	0.10	0.049^{*}
	AS > CS	0.08	0.10	1.000

$*p < 0.05$, $**p < 0.01$, $***p < 0.001$; AS: Autonomy support group, ES: Emotional support group, CS: Cognitive support group;

In specific, in viewing the changes in EFL students' self-confidence, the mean difference between autonomy support group and emotional support group was 0.50 and it was turned out to be statistically significant ($p = 0.000$). It showed that autonomy support can be more effective in enhancing EFL students' self-confidence than emotional support. Moreover, the mean difference between the autonomy support group and the cognitive support group also demonstrated a significant difference ($MD = 0.28$, $p = 0.026$). That is, autonomy support plays a more significant effect than cognitive support in improving EFL students' self-confidence in a blended learning environment. However, no statistically significant differences were found in the mean difference between the cognitive support group and the emotional support groups in the post-survey ($MD = 0.22$, $p = 0.108$). That is, when teacher's cognitive support and emotional support are given to EFL students respectively, the improvement in students' self-confidence turns out to be homogeneous.

In order to establish an autonomy-supportive environment, teachers give students enough freedom and support in arranging academic tasks and choosing learning content and problem-solving methods to enhance students' autonomy (Lam et al., 2009; Patall et al., 2010). It is also necessary to provide appropriate opportunities for students' academic activities (Skinner & Belmont, 1993). Findings in the current study showed that teacher's autonomy support could provide Chinese EFL students with more self-confidence compared with teacher's cognitive support and emotional support. Under autonomy support, it might be more possible to realize students' autonomy, which in turn satisfies their basic needs, and finally promote more self-confidence and engagement.

The results showed that only teacher autonomy support demonstrates significant improvement in their self-confidence compared with emotional support and cognitive support. EFL students can benefit more from autonomy support than from the other two types of teacher support. There is no significantly different effect in improving students' self-confidence between cognitive support and emotional support.

In terms of EFL students' anxiety in language learning, some statistically significant differences between groups were also found. Specifically, the mean differences between the emotional support group and the cognitive support group had statistically significant differences ($MD = 0.33$, $p = 0.005$), indicating that emotional support could be more effective in reducing EFL students' language anxiety compared to cognitive support. In addition, a statistical significance in the mean difference can also be found between the emotional support group and the autonomy support group ($MD = 0.25$, $p = 0.049$), which meant that teacher's emotional support is more effective in easing EFL students' language anxiety than autonomy support. However, no significant difference was found between the cognitive support group and the autonomy support group ($MD = 0.08$, $p > 0.05$), which revealed that cognitive support and autonomy support have similar effects in buffering EFL students' language anxiety under a blended learning environment.

It can be concluded that teacher's emotional support is more effective in relieving EFL students' language anxiety compared to teacher's autonomy support and cognitive support respectively. In the context of foreign language learning, although blended learning has proved positively influencing EFL students' learning engagement and language achievement, there are also voices arguing that there is no statistically significant change in EFL students' language anxiety no matter they were in a blended learning environment or conventional classroom learning environment (Bailey et al., 2017; Pae, 2007). Therefore, it would be more objective and direct to explore the influence of teacher support on students' language anxiety.

Considering the previous results in the first two research questions, teacher emotional support did not have significant effects in improving students' learning engagement and listening proficiency under the blended learning environment. While it performed a significant effect in reducing students' language anxiety. This could be attributed to that students still have a call for more emotional concern even they were given more autonomy support and cognitive support under a blended learning environment. Findings in the current study may lend support from Liu et al. ' s (2017) study which stated that students perceived their teacher's emotional support at a lower level compared to autonomy support and cognitive support.

Contrary to students who had a high perception level of teacher's emotional support, students in an online learning environment were easier to feel isolated (Sun & Sun, 2011). Although a blended learning environment addresses some of the shortcomings of both online and classroom learning, there are still a few defects being remained. Without the emotional support from teachers, students who only received autonomy support and cognitive support may still feel isolated to some extent. It was also confirmed by Liu et al. (2017) who stated that teachers pay more attention to arranging learning task, designing activities to support learner's autonomy, and supporting students' cognitive activities while pay less attention to thinking about how to communicate with their students and provide more effective emotion support to them (Liu et al., 2017).

In addition, teacher's emotional support has been confirmed that have a significant effect in reducing students' language anxiety (Piechurska-Kuciel, 2011). He stated that students rely not only on their teacher's information or appraisal support but also on their teacher's emotional support. It is said that emotional support has been reported to be a major individual predictor of students' academic achievement, especially for primary school children (Malecki & Demaray, 2003). Although young adult students are more mature and able to control their emotions and are more likely to turn to their teacher's instrumental, evaluative and informational support, teacher's emotional support may still be critical for older students, especially for students who develop negative emotions as a result of the language learning process and for whom teacher support can still alleviate these negative emotions (Piechurska-Kuciel, 2011).

Overall, in terms of EFL students' self-confidence, EFL students' can benefit more from autonomy support than from emotional support and cognitive support under a blended learning environment. As for language learning anxiety, emotional support can demonstrate more significant effects in alleviating EFL students' language anxiety in comparison to cognitive support and autonomy support in a blended learning environment.

3. Effects of Teacher Support on EFL Students' Listening Proficiency in a Blended Learning Environment

1) Changes in EFL Students' Listening Proficiency

To examine the effects of teacher support in EFL students' listening proficiency, pre-test and post-test were performed on all three groups. Paired sample t-tests were used to compare the data in the pre-test and post-test. Results of the descriptive statistics and t-tests were shown in Table 4-12.

As shown, the positive effects of teacher support on EFL listening proficiency were confirmed. After receiving teacher support, all experimental groups significantly improved their listening proficiency ($p < 0.05$). Specifically, for the emotional support group, the participants showed significant improvements in English listening proficiency ($t = 6.833$, $p = 0.000$). The mean pre-test score was 104.82 and the mean post-test score was 167. 86. Likewise, the cognitive support group significantly improved their listening proficiency from 110.95 in the pre-test to 210.77 in the post-test (t =7.733, p =0.000). In the autonomy support group, participants scored 108.14 in the pre-test while 201.00 in the post-test. The changes in mean scores were statistically significant (t = 8.286, p =0.000).

Table 4-12 Effects of Teacher Support on EFL Students' Listening Proficiency

Group	CET-4 Listening Score				t	p
	Pre-Test		Post-Test			
	M	SD	M	SD		
ES	104.82	29.73	167.86	44.35	6.833	0.000***
CS	110.95	39.35	210.77	39.11	7.733	0.000***
AS	108.14	34.90	201.00	39.04	8.286	0.000***

* $p < 0.05$, ** $p < 0.01$, *** $p < 0.001$

Considering participants' improvement in listening proficiency, it can be confirmed that all types of teacher support are effective in enhancing Chinese EFL students' listening proficiency in a blended learning environment. The findings of the current study are consistent with Kazemi et al.'s (2016) study suggesting that teacher support has a vital role in improving students' language performance. To be specific, the improvement of the emotional support group corroborates Wentzel et al.'s (2010) study proving that students can benefit from their teachers' emotional support. This study also confirmed the positive effects of cognitive support on language learning, as Kazemi et al. (2016) suggested. Moreover, the results of the current study are in line with Dincer et al.'s (2012) study confirming that students can improve their learning achievements when their teacher creates an autonomous environment. Although some of the previous studies were not directly related to English listening proficiency, all of them were related to students' learning achievements and EFL students' learning achievements, which indicates similar results on the effect of teacher support on EFL students' language achievement. Overall, these findings support Liu et al.'s (2017) study suggesting that autonomy support, emotional support, and cognitive support can play a positive role in enhancing students' academic achievement.

2) *Group Difference in EFL Students' Listening Proficiency*

The current study also investigated whether there were any differential effects of teacher support based on its types. As can be seen from Table 4-13, there was no statistically significant group difference observed in the listening pre-test. Students' listening proficiency turned out to be homogeneous among the three groups ($F = 0.171$, $p > 0.05$), which means that all participants were at a similar level of English listening proficiency level before the treatment.

Table 4-13 Pre-Test Scores on Listening Proficiency

	CET-4	AS (n = 22)		ES (n = 22)		CS (n = 22)		*F*	*p*
		M	SD	M	SD	M	SD		
Pre-Test	Listening	108.14	34.90	104.82	29.73	110.95	39.35	0.171	0.844

* AS: Autonomy support group; ES: Emotional support group;
CS: Cognitive support group

The emotional support group, cognitive support group, and autonomy support group were homogeneous in terms of their listening proficiency at the beginning of the study, as can be seen from the previous section. Therefore, one-way ANOVA was adopted again to explore whether there were any significant differences between the groups in the EFL students' post-listening test.

As demonstrated in Table 4-14, a statistically significant difference was found for the post-test among the three groups ($F = 6.649$, $p = 0.002$). In other words, the effects of teacher support on EFL listening proficiency varied depending on its type. To detect the significant differences between groups, a post hoc test with Bonferroni was applied.

Table 4-14 One-Way ANOVA for the Listening Post-Test

		Sum of Squares	*df*	Mean Square	*F*	*p*
Listening Post-Test	Between Groups	22254.58	2	11127.29	6.649	0.002**
	Within Groups	105432.46	63	1673.53		
	Total	127687.03	65			

** $p < 0.01$

As can be seen from Table 4-15, the results of the Bonferroni post hoc test revealed that the mean difference between the cognitive support group and the emotional support group was also statistically significant ($MD = 42.91$, $p = 0.003$). In the post-listening test, the cognitive support group scored higher than the emotional support group. That is, cognitive support plays a more positive role in enhancing EFL students' listening proficiency in comparison to emotional support.

Table 4-15 Results of Bonferroni Post Hoc Test on Listening Proficiency Post-Survey

Groups	MD	*SE*	*p*
CS > ES	42.91	12.33	0.003**
CS > AS	9.77	12.33	1.000
AS > ES	33.14	12.33	0.028*

$* p < 0.05$, $** p < 0.01$, $*** p < 0.001$

Interestingly, although it was found that the mean score of the post-listening test in the cognitive support group was slightly higher than that in the autonomy support group (CS: M = 210.77, AS: M = 201) (Table 4-12), no significant difference was shown between the cognitive support group and the autonomy support group. That is, cognitive support and autonomy support were equally effective on EFL students' listening proficiency.

The autonomy support group received a higher score than the emotional support group. The mean difference between the autonomy support group and the emotional support group was 33.14, which was also found to be statistically significant ($p = 0.028$). That is, autonomy support is more effective than emotional support in increasing EFL listening proficiency. Therefore, when comparing autonomy support with emotional support, teacher's autonomy support has more influence on EFL students' listening proficiency.

The findings of this study were in line with the previous research (Liu et al., 2017) suggesting that autonomy support is more effective than emotional support. The autonomy support group had more options to choose from regarding curriculum management, task design and learning resources. According to Black and Deci (2000), when students receive autonomy support from their teacher, they become more autonomous during course learning and show better learning achievement. Dincer et al. (2012) also suggested that students who receive more autonomy support from the teacher have higher levels of language proficiency and show better performance in learning.

Considering the effectiveness of teacher autonomy support, EFL teachers could focus more on the support to students' learning autonomy when preparing and designing a blended listening course. For example, to enhance students' autonomy of choice and satisfy their need for autonomy (Deci & Ryan, 2012). EFL teachers could take students' language proficiency level into consideration in their instruction, thus enriching the online academic resources. In addition, teachers could give students more choice and decision rights in course tasks and assignments based on students' own language proficiency (Liu et al., 2017).

The current study also found that Chinese EFL students benefited more from cognitive support than emotional support regarding listening proficiency. However, previous studies have shown mixed findings on this issue. For example, Liu et al. (2017) found that emotional support was more influential than cognitive support when it comes to students' learning. Rajuan et al. (2008) confirmed that cognitive support was as important as emotional support.

According to Taras (2010), teachers' cognitive support can help students regulate their learning through self-monitoring, self-evaluation of their performance, and self-reflection to identify future directions. This can promote students' autonomy and motivation in their language learning process (Xiang et al., 2021). Wu et al. (2020) also argued that teachers' cognitive support positively influences students' academic achievement.

Although the results of the previous research were different, the potential of cognitive support has been neglected (Elliott, 1995). The current study provides insight into the effects of teachers' cognitive support in EFL learning. For example, teachers could provide listening content and activities from shallow to deep (Chai & Gong, 2013) in both the face-to-face classroom and the online learning phase, which could guide students to further study. Meanwhile, it is also necessary for teachers to provide language learning skills in the classroom environment (Chai & Gong, 2013) and afford enough help to students in mastering the online learning management system or relevant applications (Hoi & Mu, 2020).

第五章　结论及建议

在语言学习中,语言能力的提高是最终目标,而听力水平则被视为外语语境中有效沟通的基础。学生的学习投入和学习成就受到个人因素和环境因素的影响,教师支持作为外在环境因素中的重要因素之一,直接影响着学生英语学习的效果。因此,教师支持是本研究的重点。本章总结了在混合学习环境下,不同类型的教师支持对中国英语学生在学习投入、语言学习态度和听力水平方面所产生的影响,同时也对混合式英语教学的改进提出了参考建议。

Chapter 5 Conclusion and Suggestion

In the context of language learning, language proficiency is the ultimate goal of language learning (Nisbet et al., 2005) and listening proficiency is viewed as the basis of effective communication in the Chinese EFL context (Deng, 2015). As students' learning engagement and achievement can be influenced by both personal and environmental factors. Teacher support, as one of the most important environmental factors which could directly influence students' learning effects, is the focus of the current study. Effects of teaching methods and instructional strategies have been discussed a lot either in a traditional face-to-face learning environment or in an online learning environment. Blended learning has been a prevalent instructional method in higher education (Kim & Yoon, 2021) and has been implemented to enhance language learners' learning engagement and achievement (Grgurovic, 2011; Yoon & Lee, 2010). Therefore, it is needed to examine whether teacher support can improve Chinese EFL students' listening proficiency under a newly prevalent learning environment.

Meanwhile, with the positive influence of teacher support on students' learning engagement, it would be more significant to examine its effects on EFL students' behavioral engagement, cognitive engagement, and emotional engagement under a blended learning environment, which would be supplementary for the effects of teacher support in the EFL context. Moreover, learning attitude has become an important factor affecting the effectiveness of language learners' learning (Krashen, 1986). The current study conducted different types of teacher support under the same blended learning environment. Effects of teacher support on Chinese EFL students' learning engagement, language learning attitude, and listening proficiency were concluded in this chapter.

1. Conclusion

The current study aimed to investigate the effects of three types of teacher support, emotional support, cognitive support, and autonomy support, on Chinese EFL students' learning engagement, language learning attitude, and English listening proficiency. Results of the current study support previous studies. Under a blended learning environment, teacher support can be an effective path for EFL students to engage in language learning (Dincer et al., 2019; He, 2009), improve their learning attitude (Olani et al., 2010; Piechurska-Kuciel, 2011; Wentzl, 1998), and promote their language proficiency (Ginaya et a., 2018; Yu et al., 2016).

Firstly, given the effects of three types of teacher support on Chinese EFL students' learning engagement in a blended learning environment, different changes were found when comparing students' three dimensions of learning engagement level before and after the experiment. Teacher's emotional support can significantly improve EFL students' behavioral engagement, cognitive engagement, and emotional engagement. However, teacher's cognitive support and autonomy support can only significantly influence EFL students' behavioral engagement and cognitive engagement.

Regarding the different effects among the three types of teacher support in improving EFL students' behavioral engagement, cognitive engagement, and emotional engagement, it was found that teacher's autonomy support is more effective in enhancing Chinese EFL students' behavioral engagement than teacher's cognitive support in a blended learning environment. Teacher's cognitive support is more influential than teacher's emotional support and autonomy support in improving students' cognitive engagement. It also revealed that teacher's emotional support, cognitive support, and autonomy support have a similar effect in promoting students' emotional engagement in a blended learning environment.

Secondly, regarding the effects of teacher support on Chinese EFL students' language learning attitude in a blended learning environment, the changes showed that teacher's emotional support, cognitive support, and autonomy support are all significantly effective in improving Chinese EFL students' self-confidence and in relieving EFL students' language anxiety. Moreover, regarding the different effects of three types of teacher support in promoting Chinese EFL students' language learning attitude, the current study showed that Chinese EFL students benefit more from teacher's autonomy support than from teacher's cognitive support and emotional support on their self-confidence. In addition, as for Chinese EFL students' language anxiety, the more support they perceive, the less anxiety they will experience. Findings in the current study showed that students' language anxiety will be significantly reduced with the help of teacher's emotional support than that under teacher autonomy support and cognitive support. However, teacher's autonomy support and cognitive support have a similar effect in buffering Chinese EFL students' language anxiety in a blended learning environment.

Thirdly, when comes to the effects of teacher support on Chinese EFL students' listening proficiency in a blended learning environment, findings firstly indicated that teacher's emotional support, cognitive support and autonomy support all have a positive effect in promoting Chinese EFL students' listening proficiency. As for the effect between different teacher support on Chinese EFL students' listening proficiency, findings showed that students gain more effective improvement from their teacher's autonomy support and cognitive support on their listening proficiency than teacher's emotional support.

The current study revealed the differential effects of teacher support on EFL students' learning engagement, language learning attitude, and listening proficiency by comparing the three types of teacher support: emotional support, cognitive support, and autonomy support, and regarded that it is necessary to regard teacher support as a multidimensional construct. Moreover, considering the positive effects of different types of teacher support in ablended learning environment under the EFL education context, the current study opens up the possibility of designing a blended English course with different types of teacher support.

Considering the effects of different types of teacher support on EFL students' behavioral engagement, cognitive engagement, and emotional engagement, it is needed to reflect on how to promote students' emotional engagement more effectively when designing a blended course with teachers' cognitive support and autonomy support. Meanwhile, under the blended learning environment, teachers should not only pay attention to students' in-class and out-class situations but pay more attention to promoting teacher-student interaction and providing more emotional support to students (Liu et al., 2017). Teachers actively participate in students' activities, which can establish a teacher-student friendly relationship to enhance learners' learning experience, which can not only improve students' cognitive level but also enhance their sense of belongings, so as to enhance their emotional involvement.

In addition, teacher's emotional support still plays a vital role in reducing EFL students' negative emotions, especially in their language anxiety during language learning. It is needed to help students to participate in school activities both mentally and physically from the perspective of psychology and sociology (Feldman, 1994). Meanwhile, teachers should try to design interactive online and offline teaching activities by integrating different types of teacher support based on the overall teaching objectives and process. For example, timely teacher feedback should be given to students to enhance their sense of belonging and relieve their learning anxiety (Arbaugh, 2001; Feidakis et al., 2014).

Moreover, considering the effect of teacher support on EFL students' listening proficiency, it also showed that teacher emotional support needs to be strengthened, especially under a blended learning environment. As students who perceived their teacher's help and support better reported higher levels in all dimensions of engagement than those who felt that teachers provided little support (Tas,2016). In order to promote language students' learning achievement, EFL teachers may add appropriate supportive behaviors which could achieve the maximum effect in different phases of the blended learning environment. Based on SDT, EFL students' autonomy and competence can be improved and satisfied if teachers could help students master and apply relevant language strategies and encourage them to raise questions in a face-to-face learning phase and supply students enough learning resources and different evaluations based on their language proficiency in the online learning phase. Once the students' basic needs for autonomy, competence, and relatedness are satisfied, their learning achievement will be enhanced approximately (Black & Deci, 2000).

2. Limitations and Suggestions

The current study, however, is constrained by several limitations. The limitations and suggestions for future research are listed below. First, the study was conducted only in the Chinese EFL context with a small number of English major students, which indicates theresults of the current study cannot be generalized to a wider population. Different results may be obtained in different EFL contexts and with a larger number of participants. In order to obtain a more generalized result, it is necessary for the future study to investigate the effects of teacher support in different EFL settings, possibly with a longer treatment period.

Secondly, although participants in the current study were randomly divided into three different groups, the initial differences of their listening proficiency and engagement levels in each group were not taken into consideration because of the small scale of participants. Students may perceive teacher support differently and thus achieve different learning effects because they have different levels of language proficiency and learning engagement. Therefore, it is necessary to investigate whether students with different language proficiency or different learning engagement level perform different effects when different teacher support is given.

Third, the current study investigated the effects of different types of teacher support. It is assumed that combining different types of teacher support in a blended course may get more effective learning outcomes. It could be further investigated what is the effect of teacher support as a comprehensive element in a blended learning environment.

Fourth, the current study only explored the direct effects of teacher support on Chinese EFL students' learning engagement, listening proficiency, and learning attitude. The relationship between the dependent variables under the influence of different types of teacher support needs to be further investigated.

Last but not least, the current study is an empirical research based on students' reported surveys and students' proficiency tests. It might be more significant if students' interviews about their perceptions of teacher support are combined in the future study. It might provide EFL teachers with more perspectives in designing blended English courses with effective teacher support.

References

Abdulrahman, T., Basalama, N., & Widodo, M. R. (2018). The impact of podcasts on EFL students' listening comprehension. International *Journal of Language Education*, 2 (2), 23-33.

Adalikwu, C. (2012). *How to Build Self-confidence, Happiness and Health.* Bloomington: Author House.

Adas, D., & Bakir, A. (2013). Writing difficulties and new solutions: Blended learning as an approach to improve writing abilities. *International Journal of Humanities and Social Science*, 3 (9), 254-266.

Agustin, N. I. W. (2019). *Students' engagement in a blended learning instruction in an EFL classroom.* [Doctoral dissertation, University Pendidikan Indonesia]. Core.

Ahmad, S. Z. (2016). The flipped classroom model to develop Egyptian EFL students' listening comprehension. *English Language Teaching*, 9 (9), 166-178.

Ahmad, S. Z. (2019). Digital posters to engage EFL students and develop their reading comprehension. *Journal of Education and Learning*, 8 (4), 169-184.

Albiladi, W. S., & Alshareef, K. K. (2019). Blended learning in English teaching and learning: A review of the current literature.

Journal of Language Teaching and Research, 10 (2), 232-238.

Allen, E., & Seaman, J. (2013). *Changing course: Ten years of tracking online education in the United States.* Sloan Consortium.

Alrabai, F. (2021). The influence of autonomy-supportive teaching on EFL students' classroom autonomy: An experimental intervention. *Frontiers in Psychology*, 12. 1-15.

Alsowat, H. (2016). An EFL flipped classroom teaching model: Effects on English language higher-order thinking skills, student engagement and satisfaction. *Journal of Education and Practice*, 7 (9), 108-121.

Ansari, E. W. &Oskrochi R. (2004). What really affects health professions students satisfaction with their educational experience? Implications for practice &research. *Nurse Educ Today*, 24, 644-655.

Ansong, D., Okumu, M., Bowen, G. L., Walker, A. M., & Eisensmith, S. R. (2017). The role of parent, classmate, and teacher support in student engagement: Evidence from Ghana. *International Journal of Educational Development*, 54, 51-58.

Appleton, J. J., Christenson, S. L., Kim, D., & Reschly, A. L. (2006). Measuring cognitive and psychological engagement: Validation of the Student Engagement Instrument. *Journal of School Psychology*, 44, 427-445.

Arbaugh, J. B. (2001). How instructor immediacy behaviors affect student satisfaction and learning in web-based courses. *Business Communication Quarterly*, 64 (4), 42-54.

Arnold, J. (1999). *Affect in language learning* (*Ed.*). Cambridge University Press.

Arnold, J. , & Brown, H. D. , (1999). A Map of the Terrain. In: Arnold, J. (Ed.), *Affect in Language Learning* (pp. 1-24). Cambridge University Press.

Asakereh, A. , &Yousofi, N. (2018). Reflective thinking, self-efficacy, self-esteem and academic achievement of Iranian EFL students in higher education: Is there a relationship. *International Journal of Educational Psychology*, 7 (1), 68-89.

Assor, A. , Kaplan, H. , & Roth, G. (2002). Choice is good, but relevance is excellent: Autonomy-enhancing and suppressing teacher behaviors predicting students' engagement in school-work. *British Journal of Educational Psychology*, 72, 261-278.

Astin, A. W. (1984). Student involvement: A developmental theory for higher education. *Journal of college student personnel*, 25 (4), 518-529.

Bailey, D. , Lee, A. , Vorst, T. , & Crosthwaite, P. R. (2017). An investigation of differences and changes in L2 writing anxiety between blended and conventional English language learning context. *CALL-EJ*, 18 (1), 22-39.

Banditvilai, C. (2016). Enhancing students' language skills through blended learning. *Electronic Journal of e-Learning*, 14 (3), 220-229.

Battistich, V. , Solomon, D. , Kim, D. I. , Watson, M. , & Schaps, E. (1995). Schools as communities, poverty levels of student populations, and students' attitudes, motives, and performance: A multilevel analysis. *American Educational Research Journal*, 32 (3), 627-658.

Battistich, V. , Solomon, D. , Watson, M. , & Schaps, E. (1997). Caring school communities. *Educ Psychol*, 32, 137-151.

Black, A. E., & Deci, E. L. (2000). The effects of instructors' autonomy support and students' autonomous motivation on learning organic chemistry: A self-determination theory perspective. *Science Education*, 84 (6), 740-756.

Bonk, C. J., & Graham, C. R. (2012). *The handbook of blended learning: Global perspectives, local designs.* John Wiley & Sons.

Caplan, G. (1974). *Support systems and community mental health: Lectures on concept development*. Behavioral Publications.

Chai, X. Y., & Gong, S. Y. (2013). The development of questionnaire on perceived mathematics teacher support for middle school students. *Studies of Psychology and Behavior.* 11 (04), 511-517.

Chang, A. C. S., & Read, J. (2006). The effects of listening support on the listening performance of EFL learners. *TESOL Quarterly*, 40 (2), 375-397.

Chang, A. C. S., & Read, J. (2007). Support for foreign language listeners. *RELC Journal*, 38 (3), 375-394.

Chang, Y. C., &Bangsri, A. (2020). Thai students' perceived teacher support on their reading ability: Mediating effects of self-efficacy and sense of school belonging. *International Journal of Educational Methodology*, 6 (2), 435-445.

Cheng, X. T. (2011). *English Listening Teaching*. Foreign Language Teaching and Research Press.

Cheng, Y. (2002). Factors associated with foreign language writing anxiety. *Foreign Language Annals*, 35 , 647-656.

Cheng, Y., Horwitz, E. K., & Schallert, D. L. (1999). Language anxiety: Differentiating writing and speaking components.

Language Learning,49 ,417-446.

Chi,X. L. (2017). *A study on the effects of teacher support on college student engagement based on Self-determination theory.* [Doctoral dissertation. Tianjin University]. CNKI.

China College Student Survey. (n. d.). *Introduction.* https://ccss. applysquare.

com/index/introduction

Chong,W. H. ,Liem,G. A. D. ,Huan,V. S. ,Kit,P. Li. ,& Ang,R. P. (2018). Student perceptions of self-efficacy and teacher support for learning in fostering youth competencies: Roles of affective and cognitive engagement. *Journal of Adolescence*,68 ,1-11.

Clément,R. (1986). Second language proficiency and acculturation: An investigation of the effects of language status and individual characteristics. *Journal of Language and social Psychology*,5 (4), 271-290.

Cohen,A. D. ,Weaver,S. J. ,& Li,T. Y. (1996). *The impact of strategies-based instruction on speaking a foreign language* . Center for Advanced Research in Language Acquisition.

Cohen, L. , Manion, L. , & Morrison, K. (2002). *Research Methods in Education.* Routledge.

Connell,J. P. ,& Wellborn,J. G. (1991). Competence,autonomy,and relatedness: A motivational analysis of self-system processes. In M. R. Gunnar & L. A. Sroufe (Eds.), *Self processes and development* (pp. 43-77). Lawrence Erlbaum Associates,Inc.

Connell,J. P. ,& Wellborn,J. G. (1994). *Engagement Versus Disaffection: Motivated Patterns Of Action In The Academic Domain* . University of Rochester.

Cooper, K. S. (2013). Eliciting engagement in the high school classroom: amixed methods examination of teaching practices. *American Educational Research Journal.* 51 (2), 363-402.

Cui, G. Y. (2014). An experimental research on blended learning in the development of listening and speaking skills in China. *Southern African Linguistics and Applied Language Studies*, 32 (4), 447-460.

Deci, E. L., & Ryan, R. M. (1985). *Intrinsic Motivation and Self-determination in Human Behavior.* Kluwer Accademic/Plenum Publishers.

Deci, E. L., & Ryan, R. M. (1987). The support of autonomy and the control of behavior. *Journal of Personality and Social Psychology*, 53 (6), 1024-1037.

Deci, E. L., & Ryan, R. M. (2000). The "what" and "why" of goal pursuits: human needs and the self-determination of behavior. *Psychological Inquiry*, 11, 227-268.

Deci, E. L., & Ryan, R. M. (2012). Self-determination theory. In P. A. M. Van Lange, A. W. Kruglanski, & E. T. Higgins (Eds.), *Handbook of Theories of Social Psychology* (pp. 416-436). Sage Publications Ltd.

Deci, E. L., Connell, J. P., & Ryan, R. M. (1989). Self-determination in a work organization. *Journal of Applied Psychology*, 74, 580-590.

Deci, E. L., Hodges, R., Pierson, L., & Tomassone, J. (1992). Autonomy and competence as motivational factors in students with learning disabilities and emotional handicaps. *Journal of Learning Disabilities*, 25 (7), 457-471.

Deci, E. L., Nezlek, J., & Sheinman, L. (1981). Characteristics of the rewarder and intrinsic motivation of the rewardee. *Journal of Personality and Social Psychology*, 40 (1), 1-10.

Deci, E. L., Schwartz, A. J., Sheinman, L., & Ryan, R. M. (1981). An instrument to assess adults' orientations toward control versus autonomy with children: Reflections on intrinsic motivation and perceived competence. *Journal of Educational Psychology*, 73, 642-650.

Deng, Q. L. (2015). A study of the correlation between Chinese non-English major EFL students' metacognition, listening anxiety and listening proficiency. *Foreign Language Teaching*, 36 (5), 59-64.

Dimitrov, D. M., & Rumrill Jr, P. D. (2003). Pretest-posttest designs and measurement of change. *Work*, 20 (2), 159-165.

Dincer, A., & Yesilyurt, S. (2017). Motivation to speak English: A Self-Determination theory perspective. *PASAA: Journal of Language Teaching and Learning in Thailand*, 53, 1-25.

Dincer, A., Yesilyurt, S., & Takkac, M. (2012). The effects of autonomy-supportive climates on EFL learner's engagement, achievement and competence in English speaking classrooms. *Procedia-Social and Behavioral Sciences*, 46, 3890-3894.

Dincer, A., Yeşilyurt, S., & Noels, K. A. (2019). Self-determined engagement in language learning: The relations among autonomy-support, psychological needs, and engagement. Cumhuriyet *Uluslararas Egitim Dergisi*, 8 (4), 1130-1147.

Dörnyei, Z. (1995). On the teachability of communication strategies. *TESOL Quarterly*, 29, 55-85.

Dörnyei,Z. (2001). New themes and approaches in second language motivation research. *Annual review of applied linguistics*,21 , 43-59.

Dörnyei, Z. (2009). The L2 motivationalself system. In: Dörnyei, Z. , Ushioda, E. (Eds.), *Motivation,Language Identity and the L2 Self. Multilingual Matters* (pp. 9-42) . Clevedon.

Driscoll,M. (2002). Blended learning: Let's get beyond the hype. *E-learning*,1 (4),1-4.

Dziuban, C. , Hartman, J. , Juge, F. , Moskal, P. , & Sorg, S. (2006). Blended learning enters the mainstream. *The Handbook of Blended Learning: Global Perspectives,Local Designs* ,195-206.

Ehrman,M. E. ,Leaver,B. L. ,& Oxford,R. L. (2003). A brief overview of individual differences in second language learning. *System*,31 (3),313-330.

Elkhafaifi,H. (2005). Listening comprehension and anxiety in the Arabic language classroom. *The Modern Language Journal*,89 , 206-220.

Elliott,B. (1995). Developing relationships: Significant episodes in professional development. *Teacher and Teaching: Theory and Practice*,1 (2),247-264.

Fallah,N. (2014). Willingness to communicate in English, communication self-confidence,motivation,shyness and teacher immediacy among Iranian English-major undergraduates: A structural equation modeling approach. *Learning and Individual Differences*,30 , 140-147.

Federici,R. A. ,&Skaalvik,E. M. (2014). Students' perceptions of emotional and instrumental teacher support: Relations with motivational and emotional responses. *International Education Studies*,7 (1),21-36.

Feidakis, M., Daradoumis, T., Caball ?, S., & Conesa, J. (2014). Embedding emotion awareness into e-learning environments. *International Journal of Emerging Technologies in Learning (iJET)*,9 (7),39-46.

Feldman,K. A. (1994). What matters in college? Four critical years revisited. by Alexander W. Astin. *The Journal of Higher Education*,65 (5),615-622.

Ferrell, A. (2012). *Classroom social environments, motivational beliefs, and student engagement.* University of Southern California.

Finn, J. D. (1989). Withdrawing from school. *Review of Educational Research*,59, 117-142.

Firdmuc, J. (2016). Foreign languages and trade: Evidence from a natural experiment. *Empirical Economics*,50 (1),31-49.

Fisher,R. ,Perényi,? . ,&Birdthistle,N. (2018). The positive relationship between flipped and blended learning and student engagement, performance and satisfaction. *Active Learning in Higher Education*, 1-17.

Flowerday,T. & Schraw,G. (2000). Teacher beliefs about instructional choice: A phenomenological study. *Journal of Educational Psychology*,92 (4): 634-645

Flowerday,T. & Schraw,G. (2003). Effect of choice on cognitive and affective engagement. *The Journal of Educational Research*, 96 (4): 207-215

Flowerday,T. ,Schraw,G. ,& Stevens,J. (2004). The role of

choice and interest in reader engagement. *The Journal of Experimental Education*,72 (2): 93-114

Fong,C. J. ,& Krause,J. M. (2014). Lost confidence and potential: a mixed methods study of underachieving college students' sources of self-efficacy. *Social Psychology of Education*,17 (2), 249-268.

Fraser,B. J. (1994). Research on classroom and school climate. In D. Gabel (Ed.), *Handbook of Research on Science Teaching and Learning* (pp. 493-541). New York,NY: Macmillan.

Fredricks, J. A., Blumenfeld, P. C., & Paris, A. H. (2004). School engagement: Potential of the concept,state of the evidence. *Review of Educational Research*,74, 59-109.

Fredricks,J. A., &McColskey, W. (2012). The measurement of student engagement: A comparative analysis of various methods and student self-report instruments. In Cristenson,S. L. ,Reschly,A. L. , & Wylie,C (Eds.). *Handbook of Research on Student Engagement* (pp. 763-782). Springer.

Gagné,M. (2003). The role of autonomy support and autonomy orientation in prosocial behavior engagement. *Motivation and emotion*,27 (3),199-223.

Gan,Z. (2020). How learning motivation influences feedback experience and preference in Chinese university EFL students. *Frontiers in Psychology*,11 ,496. 1-14.

Gardner,R. C. ,&Smyihe,P. C. (1981). On the development of the attitude/motivation test battery. *Canadian Modern Language Review*,37 (3),510-525.

Garrison,R. ,& Kanuka,H. (2004). Blended learning: Uncovering its transformative potential in higher education. *Internet and Higher Education*,7 ,95-105.

Ghanbarpour,M. (2016). Willingness to communicate,linguistic self-confidence,and language-use anxiety: The Iranian EFL context. *Theory and practice in language studies*,6 (12),2265-2271.

Ghanizadeh,A. ,Amiri,A. ,& Jahedizadeh,S. (2020). Towards humanizing language teaching: Error treatment and EFL learners' cognitive,behavioral,emotional engagement,motivation,and language achievement. *Iranian Journal of Language Teaching Research*,8 (1),129-149.

Ghazizadeh,T. ,& Fatemipour,H. (2017). The effect of blended learning on EFL learners' reading proficiency. *Journal of Language Teaching and Research*,8 (3),606-614.

Gilakjani,A. P. ,& Ahmadi,M. R. (2011). A study of factors affecting EFL learners' English listening comprehension and the strategies for improvement. Journal of Language *Teaching and Research*,2 (5),977-988.

Ginaya,G. ,Rejeki,I. N. M. ,& Astuti,N. N. S. (2018). The effects of blended learning to students' speaking ability. International Journal of Linguistics, *Literature and Culture*,4 (3),1-14.

Goodenow,C. (1993). Classroom belonging among early adolescent students: Relationships to motivation and achievement. *The Journal of Early Adolescence*,13 (1),21-43.

Gradman,H. L. ,& Hanania,E. (1991). Language learning background factors and ESL proficiency. *The Modern Language Journal*,75 (1),39-51.

Graham, C. R. (2006). Blended learning systems. *The*

Handbook of Blended Learning: Global Perspectives, Local Designs, 1, 3-21.

Graham, S. (2011). Self-efficacy and academic listening. *Journal of English for Academic Purposes*, 10 (2), 113-117.

Greene, B. A., & Miller, R. B. (1996). Influences on course performance: Goals, perceived ability, and self-regulation. *Contemporary Educational Psychology*, 21, 181-192.

Greene, B. A., Miller, R. B., Crowson, H. M., Duke, B. L., & Akey, K. L. (2004). Predicting high school students' cognitive engagement and achievement: Contributions of classroom perceptions and motivation. *Contemporary Educational Psychology*, 29 (4), 462-482.

Grgurovic, M. (2011). Blended learning in an ESL class: A case study. *Calico Journal*, 29 (1), 100-117.

Guthrie, J. T., Wigfield, A., Barbosa, P., Perencevich, K. C., Taboada, A., Davis, M. H., & Tonks, S. (2004). Increasing reading comprehension and engagement through concept-oriented reading instruction. *Journal of educational psychology*, 96 (3), 403-432.

Hagger, M. S., Chatzisarantis, N. L. D., Barkoukis, V., Wang, C. K. J., & Baranowski, J. (2005) Perceived autonomy support in physical education and leisure-time physical activity: A cross-cultural evaluation of the trans-contextual model. *Journal of Educational Psychology*, 97, 376-390.

Hannula, M. S. (2002). Attitude towards mathematics: Emotion, expectations and values. *Educational Studies in Mathematics*, 1, 25-46

Harper, S. R. & Quaye, S. J. (2009). Beyond sameness, with

engagement and outcomes for all. *Student Engagement in Higher Education.* 1-15.

Harputlu, L., & Ceylan, E. (2014). The effects of motivation and metacognitive strategy use on EFL listening proficiency. *Procedia-Social and Behavioral Sciences*, 158, 124-131.

He, Y. C. J. (2009). *Self-determination among adult Chinese English language learners: The relationship among perceived autonomy support, intrinsic motivation, and engagement.* University of Southern California.

Hein, V. (2016). Perceived autonomy support and behavioral engagement in physical education: Comment onYoo (2015). *Perceptual and Motor Skills*, 123(1), 295-299.

Henderlong, J., & Lepper, M. R. (2002). The effects of praise on children's intrinsic motivation: A review and synthesis. *Psychological Bulletin*, 128 (5), 774-795.

Hirschi, T. (1969). *Causes of delinquency.* University of California Press.

Hoi, V. N., & Mu, G. M. (2021). Perceived teacher support and students' acceptance of mobile-assisted language learning: Evidence from Vietnamese higher education context. *British Journal of Educational Technology*, 52 (2), 879-898.

Hoic-Bozic, N., Holenko Dlab, M., & Mornar, V. (2016). Recommender system and Web 2.0 tools to enhance a blended learning model. *IEEE Transactions on Education*, 59 (1), 39-44.

Horwitz, E. K., Horwitz, M. B., & Cope, J. (1986). Foreign language classroom anxiety. *The Modern Language Journal*, 70 (2), 125-132.

Hospel, V., &Galand, B. (2016). Are both classroom autonomy support and structure equally important for students' engagement? A multilevel analysis. *Learning and Instruction*, 41, 1-10.

House, J. S., Umberson, D., & Landis, K. R. (1988). Structures and processes of social support. *Annual Review of Sociology*, 14 (1), 293-318.

Hu, S. & Kuh, G. D. (2001). Being (dis)engaged in educationally purposeful activities: The influences of student and institutional characteristics. *Paper presented at the American Educational Research Association Annual Conference* (pp. 10-14). Seattle, WA.

Hu, Y. R., Liu, H. J., & Dai, D. (2019). College students' classroom learning engagement and its influencing factors from ecological perspective. *Journal of Yangzhou University* (*Higher Education Study Edition*), 20 (3), 66-70.

Huang, Q. (2016). Learners' perceptions of blended learning and the roles and interaction of f2f and online learning. *Ortesol Journal*, 33, 14-33.

Huang, R., Ma, D., & Zhang, H. (2008). Towards a design theory of blended learning curriculum. In *International Conference on Hybrid Learning and Education* (pp. 66-78). Springer, Berlin, Heidelberg.

Huang, Y. Y., Liu, C. C., Wang, Y., Tsai, C. C., & Lin, H. M. (2017). Student engagement in long-term collaborative EFL storytelling activities: An analysis of learners with English proficiency differences. *Journal of Educational Technology & Society*, 20 (3), 95-109.

Ja'ashan, M. M. N. H. (2015). Perceptions and attitudes towards blended learning for English courses: A case study of students at university of Bisha. *English Language Teaching*,8 (9),40-50.

Jackson-Kersey, R., & Spray, C. (2016). The effect of perceived psychological need support on amotivation in physical education. *European Physical Education Review*,22 (1),99-112.

Jang, H., Kim, E. J., & Reeve, J. (2012). Longitudinal test of self-determination theory's motivation mediation model in a naturally occurring classroom context. *Journal of Educational Psychology*,104 (4),1175-1188.

Jang, H., Reeve, J., & Deci, E. L. (2010). Engaging students in learning activities: It is not autonomy support or structure but autonomy support and structure. *Journal of Educational Psychology*, 102 (3),588-600.

Jang, H., Reeve, J., Ryan, R. M., & Kim, A. (2009). Can self-determination theory explain what underlies the productive, satisfying learning experiences of collectivistically oriented Koreanstudents?. *Journal of educational Psychology*,101 (3),644-661.

Jia, Z. X. (2018). *Research on college English teachers' effective teaching behaviors in blended learning.* [Doctoral dissertation. Shanghai International Studies University]. CNKI.

Jia, W. W., & Yue, C. J. (2019). Will English proficiency lead to higher starting salary? The empirical research of 2017 college graduates survey. *Education Research Monthly*,5 ,78-86.

Jiang, A. L., & Zhang, L. J. (2021). University teachers' teaching style and their students' agentic engagement in EFL learning in China: a self-determination theory and achievement goal theory integrated perspective. *Frontiers in psychology*,12 .

Jiang, Z. H., Zhao, C. L., Li, H. X., Huang, Y., & Shu, F. F. (2018b). Construction of the model of online learner-perceived teacher support behavior. *Online Learning*, 382 (11), 103-110.

Jiang, Z. H., Zhao, C. L., Li, H. X., Huang, Y., & Shu, F. F. (2018a). The power of self-regulated learning ability: Effect on learner-percevied teacher support and satisfaction. *Open Education Research*, 24 (4), 81-89.

Jimerson, S. R., Campos, E., & Grief, J. L. (2003). Toward anunderstanding of definitions and measures of school engagement and related terms. *California School Psychologist*, 8, 7-27.

Jin, G., & Wang, Y. (2019). The influence of gratitude on learning engagement among adolescents: The multiple mediating effects of teachers' emotional support and students' basic psychological needs. *Journal of Adolescence*, 77, 21-31.

Jin, Y., de Bot, K., & Keijzer, M. (2015). Factors associated with foreign language anxiety: A study of Chinese university learners of Japanese and English. *Dutch Journal of Applied Linguistics*, 4 (1), 67-85.

Jin, Y. X., & Dewaele, J. M. (2018). The effect of positive orientation and perceived social support on foreign language classroom anxiety. *System*, 74, 149-157.

Jung, Y., & Lee, J. (2018). Learning engagement and persistence in massive open online courses (MOOCS). *Computers & Education*, 122, 9-22.

Kazemi, Z., Zarehmoghadam, A., & Emami, H. (2016). The role of perceived teacher's support and motivational orientation in prediction of metacognitive awareness of reading strategies in learning

English. *Research in English Language Pedagogy*, 5 (1), 17-26.

Kelloway, E. K. (1998). *Using LISREL for structural equation modeling: a researcher's guide*. Sage.

Khajavy, G., MacIntyre, P., & Barabadi, E. (2018). Role of the emotions and classroom environment in willingness to communicate: Applying doubly latent multilevel analysis in second language acquisition research. *Studies in Second Language Acquisition*, 40 (3), 605-624.

Kiefer, S. M., Alley, K. M., & Ellerbrock, C. R. (2015). Teacher and peer support for young adolescents' motivation, engagement, and school belonging. *Rmle Online*, 38 (8), 1-18.

Kim, N. Y. (2018). A study on chatbots for developing Korean college students' English listening and reading skills. *Journal of Digital Convergence*, 16 (8), 19-26.

Kim, N. Y., & Yoon, S. Y. (2021). A comparative study on blendedbearning and flipped learning: EFL students' learner autonomy, independence, and attitudes. *Korean Journal of English Language and Linguistics*, 21, 171-188.

Kimura, M. (2000). Affective Factors of Japanese EFL Learners at JuniorColiege in the Oral Communication Tasks. *Eibeibunka: Studies in English Language, Literature and Culture*, 30, 5-19.

Kitano, K. (2001). Anxiety in the college Japanese language classroom. *The Modern Language Journal*, 85 (4), 549-566.

Klem, A. M., & Connell, J. P. (2004). Relationships matter: Linking teacher support to student engagement and achievement. *Journal of school health*, 74 (7), 262-273.

Kline, R. B. (2004). *Principles and practice of structural equation modeling* (3rd Ed.). The Guilford Press.

Krashen, S. (1982). *Principles and practice in second language acquisition.* Pergamon Press.

Kuh, G. D., Schuh, J. H., Whitt, E. J., Andreas, R. E., Lyons, J. W., Strange, C. C., Krehbiel, L. E. & MacKay, K. A. (1991). *Involving colleges: Successful approaches to fostering student learning and development outside the classroom.* Jossey-Bass.

Kuh, G. D. (2001a). The National Survey of Student Engagement: Conceptual framework and overview of psychometric properties. *Academia.*

Kuh, G. D. (2001b). Assessing what really matters to student learning: Inside the National Survey of Student Engagement. *Change*, 33 (3), 10-17, 66.

Kuh, G. D., Kinzie, J., Schuh, J. H., & Whitt, E. J. (2005). Never let it rest lessons about student success from high-performing colleges and universities. Change: *The Magazine of Higher Learning*, 37 (4), 44-51

Lam, S., Wong, B. P. H., Yang, H., & Liu, Y. (2012). Understanding student engagement with a contextual model. In S. L. Christenson, A. L. Reschly, & C. Wylie (Eds.). *Handbook of research on student engagement* (pp. 403-420). Springer.

Lam, S. F., Jimerson, S., Wong, B. P., Kikas, E., Shin, H., Veiga, F. H., ... &Zollneritsch, J. (2014). Understanding and measuring student engagement in school: The results of an international study from 12 countries. *School Psychology Quarterly*, 29 (2), 213-232.

Lam, S. F., & Law, Y. K. (2007). The roles of instructional practices and motivation in writing performance. *Journal of Experimental Education*, 75 (2), 146-164.

Lam, S. F., Cheng, R. W. Y., & Ma, W. Y. (2009). Teacher and studentintrinsic motivation in project-based learning. *Instructional Science*, 37 (6), 565-578.

Lam, S. F., Pak, T. S., & Ma, W. Y. K. (2007). Motivating instructional contexts inventory. In P. R. Zelick (Ed.), *The Psychology of Motivation* (pp. 119-136). Hauppauge, NJ: Nova Science.

Law, Y. (2011). The role of teachers' cognitive support in motivating young Hong Kong Chinese children to read and enhancing reading comprehension. *Teaching and Teacher Education*, 27 (1), 73-84.

Lawrence, D. (2006). *Enhancing self-esteem in the classroom* (3rd Ed.). Paul Chapman Publication.

Lee, E., Pate, J. A., & Cozart, D. (2015). Autonomy support for online students. *TechTrends*, 59 (4), 54-61.

Lee, V. E., Smith, J. B., Perry, T. E., & Smylie, M. A. (1999). Social support, academic press, and student achievement: A view from the middle grades in Chicago. Improving Chicago's Schools. *A Report of the Chicago Annenberg Research Project*.

Legault, L., Green-Demers, I., & Pelletier, L. (2006). Why do high school students lack motivation in the classroom? Toward an understanding of academic amotivation and the role of social support. *Journal of educational psychology*, 98 (3), 567-582.

Liu, B., Zhang, W. L., & Liu, J. L. (2017). Study on the

effect of teacher support on online Learners' learning engagement. *E-Education Research.* 11 ,63-68 +80.

Liu, H. J. ,& Chen, T. H. (2013). Foreign language anxiety in young learners: How it relates to multiple intelligences, learner attitudes, and perceived competence. *Journal of Language Teaching & Research*,4 (5). 932-938.

Liu, M. (2013). Blended learning in a university EFL writing course: Description and evaluation. *Journal of Language Teaching & Research*,4 (2),301-309.

Liu, X. M. (2016). Study on the innovative blended visual-aural-oral teaching model for college English. *Modern Educational Technology*,26 (11). 100-106.

Longcope, P. (2009). Differences between the EFL and the ESL language learning contexts. *Studies in Language and Culture*,30 (2),303-320.

Lorsbach, A. W. ,& Jinks, J. L. (1999). Self-efficacy theory and learning environment research. *Learning Environments Research*, 2 ,157-167.

Luan, L. , Hong, J. C. , Cao, M. , Dong, Y. ,& Hou, X. (2020). Exploring the role of online EFLlearners' perceived social support in their learning engagement: a structural equation model. *Interactive Learning Environments*, 1-12.

Luo, W. (2017). Perceived teaching practice and its prediction of student engagement in Singapore. *Asia Pacific Education Review*, 18 (4),451-463.

Ma, J. (2020). A study of the influencing mechanism of university student engagement in a blended learning environment. *China*

Distance Education,2 . 57-67.

Ma, J. , Cheng, J. , & Han, X. (2017). Initial development process of a student engagement scale in blended learning environment. In 2017 *International Conference of Educational Innovation through Technology* (*EITT*), 234-237.

Ma, J. ,& Zhou, Q. (2019). An empirical study on the dimensions and factors of collegestudents engagement in blended learning environment. *Research in Educational Development.* 39 (1),54-65.

MacIntyre, P. D. (2017). An overview of language anxiety research and trends in itsdevelopment. In Gkonou, C. , Daubney, M. & Dewaele, J. M. (Eds.), *New insightsinto language anxiety: Theory, research and educational implications* (pp. 11-30). Multilingual Matters.

MacIntyre, P. D. ,& Gardner, R. C. (1989). Anxiety and second - language learning: Toward a theoretical clarification. *Language Learning*,39 (2),251-275.

MacIntyre, P. D. , Noels, K. A. ,& Clegment, R. (1997). Biases in self-ratings of second language proficiency: The role of language anxiety. *Language Learning*,47 (2),265-287.

Malecki, C. K. , & Demary, M. K. (2002). Measuring perceived social support: Development of the child and adolescent social support scale (CASSS). *Psychology in the Schools*,39 (1),1-18.

Malecki, C. K. ,& Demaray, M. K. (2003). What type of support do they need? Investigating student adjustment as related to emotional, informational, appraisal, and instrumental support. *School Psychology Quarterly*,18 (3),231-252.

Marks, H. M. (2000). Student engagement in instructional activity: Patterns in the elementary, middle, and high school years. *American Educational Research Journal*,37 (1),153-184.

Massey,R. (2010). *A Q-methodological study to investigate the views of children and young people who are deaf: how adults in educational settings help to support their social and emotional wellbeing*. [Doctoral dissertation, The University of Sheffield]. EthOS.

Means,B.,Toyama,Y.,Murphy,R.,& Baki,M. (2013). The effectiveness of online and blended learning: A meta-analysis of the empirical literature. *Teachers College Record*,115 (3),1-47.

Mercer, S., & Dörnyei, Z. (2020). *Engaging language learners in contemporary classrooms.* Cambridge University Press.

Merwin,J. C. (1969). Historical view of changing concepts of evaluation. In Tyler, R. L. (Ed). *Educational evaluation: New roles, new methods. 68th yearbook of the national society for the study of education, Part II.* Chicago: University of Chicago Press.

Meyer,D. K.,& Turner,J. C. (2006). Re-conceptualizing emotion and motivation to learn in classroom contexts. *Educational Psychology Review*,18,377 - 390.

Miller,R. B.,Greene,B. A.,Montalvo,G. P.,Ravindran,B., & Nichols,J. D. (1996). Engagement in academic work: The role of learning goals, future consequences, pleasing others, and perceived ability. *Contemporary Educational Psychology*,21 (4),388-422.

Ministry of Education of the People's Republic of China (2020). *College English curriculum requirements.* Beijing: Higher Education Press.

Mirsane, M., & Khabiri, M. (2016). The effect of teaching

communicative strategy on EFL learners' willingness to communicate. *Theory and Practice in Language Studies*,6 (2),399-407.

Mitchell,S.,&DellaMattera,J. (2011). Teacher support and student's self-efficacy beliefs. *Journal of Contemporary Issues in Education*,5 (2),24-35.

Mu,S.,Qiao,J.,Cui,M.,Wang,X.,Tang,D.,Zhang,H.,& Feng,Y. (2019). How teachers' support affects learners' participation in blended learning. In *International Conference on Technology in Education* (pp. 44-53). Springer,Singapore.

Ni,H. (2012). The effects of affective factors in SLA and pedagogical implications. *Theory & Practice in Language Studies*,2 (7), 1508-1513.

Niemiec,C. P.,& Ryan,R. M. (2009). Autonomy,competence,and relatedness in the classroom: Applying self-determination theory to educational practice. *Theory and Research in Education*,7 (2),133-144.

Nisbet,D. L.,Tindall,E. R.,& Arroyo,A. A. (2005). Language learning strategies and English proficiency of Chinese university students. *Foreign Language Annals*,38 (1),100-107.

Noels,K. A.,Clément,R.,& Pelletier,L. G. (1999). Perceptions of teachers' communicative style and students' intrinsic and extrinsic motivation. *Modern Language Journal*,83 (1),23-34.

Noels,K. A.,Pelletier,L. G.,Clément,R.,& Vallerand,R. J. (2000). Why are you learning a second language? motivational orientations and self-determination theory. *Language Learning*,50 (1), 57-85.

Nordquist,R. (2020,March 26). English as a Foreign Language

(EFL). *Thoughtco*. Retrived from https://www. thoughtco. com/english-as-a-
foreign-language-efl-1690597.

Neumeier, P. (2005). A closer look at blended learning-parameters for designing a blended learning environment for language teaching and learning. *ReCALL*, 17 (02), 163-178.

Nunan, D. (1998). *Approaches to teaching listening in the language classroom*. Paper presented at the Korea TESOL Conference, Seoul.

Oga-Baldwin, W. Q. (2020). Show them how, but don't intrude: Autonomy support promotes EFL classroom attendance and achievement, teacher control hinders it. *Language Teacher*, 44, 3-10.

Olani, A., Harskamp, E., Hoekstra, R., & van der Werf, G. (2010). The roles of self-efficacy and perceived teacher support in the acquisition of statistical reasoning abilities: A path analysis. *Educational Research and Evaluation*, 16 (6), 517-528.

Oraif, I. M. K. (2018). *An investigation into the impact of the flipped classroom on intrinsic motivation (IM) and learning outcomes on an EFL writing course at a university in Saudi Arabia based on self-determination theory (SDT)*. [Doctoral dissertation, University of Leicester]. Leicester Figshare.

O'Reilly, E. N. (2014). Correlations among perceived autonomy support, intrinsic motivation, and learning outcomes in an intensive foreign language program. *Theory and Practice in Language Studies*, 4 (7), 1313-1318.

Osguthorpe, R. T., & Graham, C. R. (2003). Blended learning environments: Definitions and directions. *Quarterly Review of*

Distance Education,4 (3),227-233.

Pace,C. R. (1984). *Measuring the quality of dollege student experiences. An account of the development and use of the college student experience questionnaire*. Higher Education Research Institute.

Pae,J. K. (2007). Wiki-based English writing: Its effect on English writing proficiency and anxiety and Korean learners' perceptions. *Multimedia-Assisted Language Learning*,10 (1),81-105.

Palacios, L. M. (1998). *Foreign language anxiety and classroom environment: A study of Spanish university students.* The University of Texas at Austin.

Pan,M. W.,& Zou,S. (2020). Test for English majors in the new era: Challenges, solutions and future endeavors. *Technology Enhanced Foreign Language Education.* 2,62-68.

Papi,M. (2010). The L2 motivationalself system, L2 anxiety, and motivated behavior: A structural equation modeling approach. *System*,38 (3),467-479.

Parsons,S. A.,Nuland,L. R.,& Parsons,A. W. (2014). The ABCs of student engagement. *Phi Delta Kappan*,95 (8),23-27.

Pascarella,E. T.,Seifert,T. A.,& Blaich,C. (2010). How effective are the NSSE benchmarks in predicting important educationaloutcomes. *Change: The Magazine of Higher Learning*,42 (1),16-22.

Patall,E. A.,Cooper,H.,& Wynn,S. R. (2010). The effectiveness and relative importance of choice in the classroom. *Journal of Educational Psychology*,102 (4),896-915.

Patrick,H.,Anderman,L. H.,& Ryan,A. M. (2004). Social

motivation and the classroom environment. In C. Midgley (Ed.), *Goals, goal structures, and patterns of adaptive learning* (pp. 85-108). Malwah, NJ: Lawrence Erlbaum Associates.

Patrick, H., Ryan, A. M., & Kaplan, A. (2007). Early adolescents' perceptions of the classroom social environment, motivational beliefs, and engagement. *Journal of Educational Psychology*, 99 (1), 83-98.

Phakiti, A. (2003). A closer look at the relationship of cognitive and metacognitive strategy use to EFL reading achievement test performance. *Language Testing*, 20 (1), 26-56.

Philp, J., & Duchesne, S. (2016). Exploring Engagement in Tasks in the Language Classroom. *Annual Review of Applied Linguistics*, 36, 50-72.

Phon, S. (2017). Factors affecting the English language proficiency of students majoring in English at a rural university in Cambodia. *UC Occasional Paper Series*, 1 (1), 69-92.

Pianta, R. C., & Hamre, B. K. (2009). Conceptualization, measurement, and improvement of classroom processes: standardized observation can leverage capacity. *Educational Researcher*, 38 (2), 109-119.

Pianta, R. C., Belsky, J., Vandergrift, N., Houts, R., & Morrison, F. J. (2008). Classroom effects on children's achievement trajectories in elementary school. *American Educational Research Journal*, 45 (2), 365-397.

Piechurska-Kuciel, E. (2011). Perceived teacher support and language anxiety in Polish secondary school EFL learners. *Studies in Second Language Learning and Teaching*, 1 (1), 83-100.

Rajuan, M. , Beijaard, D. , & Verloop, N. (2008). Student teachers' perceptions of their mentors as internal triggers for learning. *Teaching Education*,19 (4),279-292.

Reeve,J. (2002). Self-determination theory applied to educational settings. In Deci,E. L. ,& Ryan,R. M. (Eds.). H*andbook of self-determination research* (pp. 183-204). Rochester,NY: University of Rochester Press.

Reeve,J. (2006). Teachers as facilitators: What autonomy-supportive teachersdo and why their students benefit. *The Elementary School Journal*,106 (3),225-236.

Reeve,J. (2009). Why teachers adopt a controlling motivating style toward students and how they can become more autonomy supportive. *Educational Psychologist*,44, 159-175.

Reeve,J. (2012). A self-determination theory perspective on studentengagement. In A. L. R. S. L. Christenson, & C. Wylie (Ed.), *Handbook of research on student engagement* (pp. 149-172). New York: Springer.

Reeve,J. , Bolt, E. , & Cai, Y. (1999). Autonomy-supportive teachers: Howthey teach and motivate students. *Journal of Educational Psychology*,91 (3),537-548.

Reeve,J. , & Jang, H. (2006). What teachers say and do to support students' autonomy during a learning activity. *Journal of Educational Psychology*,98 (1),209-218.

Reeve,J. ,& Tseng,C. M. (2011). Agency as a fourth aspect of students' engagement during learning activities. *Contemporary Educational Psychology*,36 (4),257-267.

Reeve,J. ,Jang,H. ,Carrell,D. ,Jeon,S. ,&Barch,J. (2004).

Enhancing students' engagement by increasing teachers' autonomy support. *Motivation and Emotion*, 28 (2), 147-169.

Richland, L. E., Zur, O., & Holyoak, K. J. (2007). Cognitive supports for analogies in the mathematics classroom. *Science-New York*, 316 (5828), 1128-1129.

Rimm-Kaufman, S. E., Baroody, A. E., Larsen, R. A., Curby, T. W., & Abry, T. (2015). To what extent do teacher-student interaction quality and student gender contribute to fifth graders' engagement in mathematics learning. *Journal of Educational Psychology*, 107 (1), 1-16.

Roeser, R. W., Eccles, J. S., & Sameroff, A. J. (2000). School as a context of early adolescents' academic and social-emotional development: A summary of research findings. *The Elementary School Journal*, 100 (5), 443-471.

Ruzek, E. A., Hafen, C. A., Allen, J. P., Gregory, A., Mikami, A. Y., & Pianta, R. C. (2016). How teacher emotional support motivates students: The mediating roles of perceived peer relatedness, autonomy support, and competence. *Learning and Instruction*, 42, 95-103.

Ryan, A. M., & Patrick, H. (2001). The classroom social environment and changes in adolescents' motivation and engagement during middle school. *American Educational Research Journal*, 38 (2), 437-460.

Ryan, R. M., & Deci, E. L. (2000). Self-determination theory and the facilitation of intrinsic motivation, social development, and well-being. Am. *Psychol.* 55, 68-78.

Ryan, R. M., & Deci, E. L. (2008). Self-determination theory and the role of basic psychological needs in personality and the organization of behavior. In O. P. John, R. W. Robins, & L. A. Pervin (Eds.), *Handbook of personality: Theory and research* (pp. 654-678). The Guilford Press.

Ryan, R. M., & Deci, E. L. (2012). Multiple identities within a single self. In Leary, M. R. & Tangney, J. P. (2nd Eds.). *Handbook of self and identity* (pp. 225-246). The Guilford Press.

Sadoughi, M., & Hejazi, S. Y. (2021). Teacher support and academic engagement among EFL learners: The role of positive academic emotions. *Studies in Educational Evaluation*, 70, 1-8.

Sahin-Kizil, A. (2014). Blended instruction for EFL learners: Engagement, learning and course satisfaction. *Jalt Call Journal*, 10 (3), 175-188.

Saito, Y., Garza, T. J., & Horwitz, E. K. (1999). Foreign language reading anxiety. *The Modern Language Journal*, 83, 202-218.

Sakiz, G. (2017). Perceived teacher affective support in relation to emotional and motivational variables in elementary school science classrooms in Turkey. *Research in Science & Technological Education*, 35 (1), 108-129.

Sakiz, G., Pape, S. J., & Hoy, A. W. (2012). Does perceived teacher affective support matter for middle school students in mathematics classrooms?. *Journal of school Psychology*, 50 (2), 235-255.

Sansone, C., & Harackiewicz, J. M. (Eds.). (2000). *Intrinsic and extrinsic motivation: The search for optimal motivation and performance*. Elsevier.

Sarafianou, A., & Gavriilidou, Z. (2015). The effect of strategy-based instruction on strategy use by upper-secondary Greek students of

EFL. *Electronic Journal of Foreign Language Teaching*, 12 (1), 21-34.

Scovel, T., (1978). The effect ofaffect on foreign language learning: a review of the anxiety literature. *Language Learning* 28, 129-142.

Sellers, V. D. (2000). Anxiety and reading comprehension in Spanish as a foreign language. *Foreign Language Annals*, 33 (5), 512-520.

Sha, J. R., Kan, Zh. C., & Li, W. (2020). An empirical research on the improvent of college students' school engagement by teacher support strategies in blended learning environment. *Educational Resource and Technology*. 403, 127-133.

Shih, R. C. (2010). Blended learning using video-based blogs: Public speaking for English as a second language students. *Australasian Journal of Educational Technology*, 26 (6). 883-897.

Sinatra, G. M., Heddy, B. C., & Lombardi, D. (2015). The challenges of defining and measuring student engagement in science. *Educational Psychologist*, 50 (1), 1-13.

Singh, H., & Reed, C. (2001). A white paper: Achieving success with blended learning. *Centra Software Retrieved*, 12 (3), 206-207.

Skinner, E. A. (1995). *Perceived control, motivation, and coping*. Sage Publication.

Skinner, E. A., & Belmont, M. J. (1993). Motivation in the classroom: Reciprocal effects of teacher behavior and student engagement across the school year. *Journal of Educational Psychology*, 85 (4), 571-581.

Skinner, E. A., Wellborn, J. G., & Connell, J. P. (1990). What it takes to do well in school and whether I've got it: A process model of perceived control and children's engagement and achievement in school. *Journal of Educational Psychology*, 82 (1), 22-32.

Skinner, E., Furrer, C., Marchand, G., & Kindermann, T. (2008). Engagement and disaffection in the classroom: Part of a larger motivational dynamic? *Journal of Educational Psychology*, 100 (4), 765-781.

Starks, D., &Paltridge, B. (1996). A note on using sociolinguistic methods to study non-native attitudes towards English. *World Englishes*, 15 (2), 217-224.

Stefanou, C. R., Perencevich, K. C., DiCintio, M., & Turner, J. C. (2004). Supporting autonomy in the classroom: ways teachers encourage student decision making and ownership. *Educational Psychologist*, 39, 97-110.

Stroet, K., Opdenakker, M. C., & Minnaert, A. (2013). Effects of need supportive teaching on early adolescents' motivation and engagement: A review of the literature. *Educational Research Review*, 9, 65-87.

Sun, C. Y., & Sun, S. H. (2011). A survey of online distance learners' learning engagement. *Journal of Vocational Education*, 25, 44-48.

Sun, C., Zhou, Z., Yu, Q., Gong, S., Yi, L., & Cao, Y. (2021). Exploring the effect of perceived teacher support on multiple creativity tasks: Based on the expectancy-value model of achievement motivation. *The Journal of Creative Behavior*, 55 (1), 15-24.

Sun, Z., & Qiu, X. (2017). Developing a blended learning

model in an EFL class. *International Journal of Continuing Engineering Education and Life Long Learning*,27 (1-2),4-21.

Tabrizi,H. M.,& Saeidi,M. (2015). The relationship among Iranian EFL learners' self-efficacy,autonomy and listening comprehension ability. *English Language Teaching*,8 (12),158-169.

Taras,M. (2010). Student self-assessment: Processes and consequences. *Teaching in Higher Education*,15 (2),199-209.

Tardy,C. H. (1985). Social support measurement. *American Journal of Community Psychology*,13 (2),187-202.

Tas,Y. (2016). The contribution of perceived classroom learning environment and motivation to student engagement in science. *Eur J Psychol Educ.* 31,557-577.

Tas,Y.,Subaş,M.,& Yerdelen,S. (2019). The role of motivation between perceived teacher support and student engagement in science class. *Educational Studies*,45 (5),582-592.

Tinto,V. (1975). Dropout from higher education: A theoretical synthesis of recent research. *Review of Educational Research*,45 (1),89-125.

Trickett,E. J.,& Moos,R. H. (1973). Social environment of junior high and high school classrooms. *Journal of Educational Psychology*,65 (1),93-102.

Tridinanti,G. (2018). The correlation between speaking anxiety,self-confidence,and speaking achievement of Undergraduate EFL students of private university in Palembang. *International Journal of Education and Literacy Studies*,6 (4),35-39.

Trowler,V. (2010). Student engagement literature review. *The Higher Education Academy*,11 (1),1-15.

Truitt, S. N. (1995). *Anxiety and beliefs about language learning: A study of Korean university students learning English.* [Doctoral dissertation, The University of Texas]. ProQuest Dissertations Publishing.

Vallerand, R. J., Fortier, M. S., & Guay, F. (1997). Self-determination and persistence in a real-life setting: toward a motivational model of high school dropout. *Journal of Personality and Social psychology*, 72 (5), 1161-1176.

Vaughan, N. (2014). Student engagement and blended learning: Making the assessment connection. *Education Sciences*, 4 (4), 247-264.

Vogely, A. J. (1998). Listening comprehension anxiety: Students' reported sources and solutions. *Foreign Language Annals*, 31, 67-80.

Wang, M. T., & Eccles, J. S. (2013). School context, achievement motivation, and academic engagement: A longitudinal study of school engagement using a multidimensional perspective. *Learning and Instruction*, 28, 12-23.

Wang, N., Chen, J., Tai, M., & Zhang, J. (2019). Blended learning for Chinese university EFL learners: Learning environment and learner perceptions. *Computer Assisted Language Learning*, 34 (3), 297-323.

Way, N., Reddy, R., & Rhodes, J. (2007). Students' perceptions of school climate during the middle school years: Associations with trajectories of psychological and behavioral adjustment. *American Journal of Community Psychology*, 40 (3-4), 194-213.

Wei, D., Zhang, D., He, J., & Bobis, J. (2020). The impact of perceived teachers' autonomy support on students' mathematics achievement: evidences based on latent growth curve modelling. *European Journal of Psychology of Education*, 35 (3), 703-725.

Wentzel, K. R. (1994). Relations of social goal pursuit to social acceptance, classroom behavior, and perceived social support. *Journal of Educational psychology*, 86 (2), 173-182.

Wentzel, K. R. (1998). Social relationships and motivation in middle school: The role of parents, teachers, and peers. *Journal of Educational Psychology*, 90 (2), 202-209.

Wentzel, K. R. (2017). Peer relationships, motivation, and academic performance at school. In A. J. Elliot, C. S. Dweck, & D. S. Yeager (Eds.), *Handbook of competence and motivation: Theory and application* (pp. 586-603). The Guilford Press.

Wentzel, K. R., Battle, A., Russell, S. L., & Looney, L. B. (2010). Social supports from teachers and peers as predictors of academic and social motivation. *Contemporary Educational Psychology*, 35 (3), 193-202.

Wentzel, K. R., Russell, S., & Baker, S. (2016). Emotional support and expectations from parents, teachers, and peers predict adolescent competence at school. *Journal of Educational Psychology*, 108 (2), 242-255.

Whitelock, D. D., &Jelfs, A. (2003). Editorial: Journal of Educational Media special issue on blended learning. *Journal of Educational Media*, 28 (2-3), 99-100.

Wigfield, A., Guthrie, J. T., Perencevich, K. C., Taboada, A., Klauda, S. L., McRae, A., et al. (2008). Role of reading engagement in mediating the effects of reading comprehension instruction on reading outcomes. *Psychology in the Schools*,45 ,432-445.

Wu,H. J. ,Ge,W. S. ,& He,J. H. (2020). Effect ofteachr support on the learning persistence of MOOC: Based on S-O-R and TAM perspective. *Modern Distance Education*, (03),89-96.

Xiang,X. ,Yuan,R. ,& Yu,B. (2021). Implementing assessment as learning in the L2 writing classroom: a Chinese case. *Assessment & Evaluation in Higher Education* ,1-15.

Xu,J. F. & Fan,Y. M. (2019). Foreign language learners' engagement under the social cognitive perspective. *Foreign Language Education*. 40 (5),39-43.

Xu,Y. ,& Carless,D. (2016). 'Only true friends could be cruelly honest': cognitive scaffolding and social-affective support in teacher feedback literacy. *Assessment & Evaluation in Higher Education*,42 (7),1082-1094.

Yamashita,J. (2002). Mutual compensation between L1 reading ability and L2 language proficiency in L2 reading comprehension. *Journal of Research in Reading*,25 (1),81-95.

Yan Q. Z. ,Gu X. D. (2020). Investigating English Majors' English Language Proficiency at the Foundation Stage: Based on the CEFR. *Foreign Language in China* , 17 (4). 69-76.

Yang,L. J. & Han,X. L. (2013). Trends and characteristics of college students' learning engagement: An analysis based on on-campus tracking data. *Fudan Education Forum*,11 (5),46-52.

Yeung,R. ,&Leadbearer,B. (2010). Adults make a difference: The protective effects of parent and teacher emotional support on emotional and behavioral problems of peer-victimized adolescents. *Journal of Community Psychology*,38 (1),80-98.

Yeldham, M. (2016). Second language listening instruction: Comparing a strategies - based approach with an interactive, strategies/bottom - up skills approach. *Tesol Quarterly*, 50 (2), 394-420.

Yesilyurt, S. (2008). The relationship between students' perceived autonomy support and motivational patterns in English writing courses: A self-determination theory approach. *Atatürk ? niversitesi Sosyal Bilimler Enstitüsü Dergisi*, 12 (2), 397-412.

Yildirim, S. (2012). Teacher support, motivation, learning, strategy use, and achievement: a multilevel mediation model. *J Exp Educ*, 80, 150-172.

Yoo, J. (2015). Perceived autonomy support and behavioral engagement in physical education: A conditional process model of positive emotion and autonomous motivation. *Perceptual and motor skills*, 120 (3), 731-746.

Yoon, S. Y., & Lee, C. H. (2010). The perspectives and effectiveness of blended learning in L2 writing of Korean university students. *Multimedia Assisted Language Learning*, 13 (2), 177-204.

Yu, B., & Shen, H. (2012). Predicting roles of linguistic confidence, integrative motivation and second language proficiency on cross-cultural adaptation. *International Journal of Intercultural Relations*, 36 (1), 72-82.

Yu, X. (2016). The status quo of English teaching in China: An EFLperspective. *Foreign Language Teaching Theory and Practice*, (3). 37-42.

Yuan, J. M. & Kim, C. M. (2017). The effects of autonomy support on student engagement in peer assessment. *Educational Technology Research and Development*, 66, 1-28.

Yue, Q. X. , & Lu, H. D. (2014). Intervention of teachers' emotional support perceived by senior high school students. *Educational Measurement and Evaluation*, 6, 47-51.

Zare-ee, A. (2007). The relationship between cognitive and meta-cognitive strategy use and EFL reading achievement. *Journal of Applied Psychology*, 2 (5), 105-119.

Zhang, R. , Yuan, L. M. (2004). Research on relationship between learninganxiety, self-efficacy and English performance. *Psychological Development and Education.* 3, 56-61.

Zhang, W. , & Zhu, C. (2018). Comparing learning outcomes of blended learning and traditional face-to-face learning of university students in ESL courses. *International Journal on E-Learning*, 17 (2), 251-273.

Zhang, X. , Dai, S. , &Ardasheva, Y. (2020). Contributions of (de) motivation, engagement, and anxiety to English listening and speaking. *Learning and Individual Differences*, 79, 101856.

Zhang, Y. (2009). *The implementation of the blended learning approach in college English classroom.* [Doctoral dissertation, Shanghai International Studies Universy]. CNKI.

Zhao, Ch. L. , Li, H. X. , Jiang, Z. H. , & Huang, Y. (2018). Alleviating online learners' burnout: A study on the influence of teachers' emotional support. *Distance Education and Online Learning*, 2, 29-36.

Zhuang, Z. X. , & Chen G. (2017). Problems in English major education in China and its counter measures and thoughts. *Foreign Language World*, 3, 9-15.

Zou S. , Fang X. C. , & Chen W. (2012). Analysis on TEM-4

and TEM-8 in 2011, *Foreign Language Testing and Teaching*, 1, 1-10.

Zou, B. (2013). Teachers' support in using computers for developing students' listening and speaking skills in pre-sessional English courses. *Computer Assisted Language Learning*, 26 (1), 83-99.

Appendix

Appendix 1. Questionnaire

This survey is to understand your learning engagement level and learning attitude while learning a blended English course. Data collected through this questionnaire will remain confidential. For each statement below, mark with a tick (√) according to your experience or feeling. There is no right and wrong answer. The survey will take no longer than 15 minutes. Thankyour for your time.

· Please choose the most suitable answer based on your performance in blended course.

Items	1 = Never 2 = Seldom 3 = Sometimes 4 = Often 5 = Always				
	1	2	3	4	5
1. I actively raise my points in team communication					
2. I seek advice from instructor on the web-based learning system when I encounter difficulties in blended learning					

3. I reply other students question on the web-based learning system discussion forum					
4. I complete my responsibilities in group work in time					
5. I used web-based learning system or other instant message applications to communicate with other students about English learning					
6. I share English learning resources and information with my classmates on the web-based learning system or through instant message applications					
7. I work with other students on difficult tasks in team activities					
8. I discuss with instructor face-to-face when I encounter difficulties in blended learning environment					
9. I make sure I keep up with the weekly learning activities and tasks in time in blended learning environment					
10. I try my best to understand what the instructor teaches in blended learning environment					
11. I reflect on learning content and write summary notes after class					
12. I actively respond to topic instructor post on the discussion forum					
13. I preview learning materials before the class					
14. I set learning plan for myself in order to direct my activities in blended learning					

15. I use what I have learned to solve practical language problems in blended course					
16. I make connections between things that I have learned in blendedlearning					
17. I have clear learning goals in every stage of blended learning					
18. I make good use of my study time for this blended learning course					
19. I connect what I have learned in this course with other subject in blended learning					
20. I ask myself questions and think through a topic when I am reading learning materials in blended learning					
21. I use what I have learned from assignments and tests to promote my next step of learning					
22. I think about what I have already learned to understand a new topic in blended learning					
23. Blended learning could stimulate my enthusiasm for English learning					
24. I am interested in this English blended learning course					
25. I feel myself as a member of the group in the blended learning					
26. I feel excited when we start a new topic in blended learning					
27. I feel pleasure when learning this blended English course					

· Please choose the most suitable answer according to you real feeling in English learning.

Items	1 = Totally Disagree 2 = Disagree 3 = Uncertain 4 = Agree 5 = Totally Agree				
	1	2	3	4	5
1. I am sure about my ability to do the assignments in class (both online and offline)					
2. Compared to others in this class, I think I am good at learning English					
3. I am certain I can understand the material presented in class					
4. I am sure I can do as well as, or better than, other students in this class on exams					
5. I am sure I have the ability to understand the ideas and skills taught in this course					
6. Compared with other students in this class my English learning and study skills are strong					
7. I am certain I can learn the ideas and skills taught in this class					

· Please choose the most suitable answer according to you real feeling in using English.

Table 4-15 Results of Bonferroni Post Hoc Test on Listening Proficiency Post-Survey

Items	1 = Never 2 = Seldom 3 = Sometimes 4 = Often 5 = Always				
	1	2	3	4	5
1. I feel tense if a foreigner asked me for directions in English					
2. I feel uneasy when speaking English with a n-ative speaker					
3. I become nervous and confused when I am speaking in my English class					
4. I am afraid of sounding stupid in English be-cause of the mistake I made					
5. I am worried that other speakers of English would find my English strange					
6. I am afraid that other students will laugh at me when I speak English.					